AF230419

Fire in the Temple

Fire in the Temple

A Play
by Glen Williamson

SteinerBooks | 2025

Published by SteinerBooks | Anthroposophic Press
834 Main Street, PO Box 358
Spencertown, New York 12165

www.steinerbooks.org

ISBN: 978-1-62148-396-0

DEDICATED TO MICAH EVERETT MCMANUS

October 2, 2019–November 30, 2022

The premiere of FIRE IN THE TEMPLE *took place
on September 15, 2023, in Fountain Hall,
at Camphill USA, Copake, New York,
directed by John McManus.*

Preface

In 1981, as a young student of theater and anthropology, I was sent, through an exchange program, to work as a stagehand on a full production of Goethe's Faust at the Goetheanum, a massive strangely-shaped concrete theater building on a hill in Dornach, Switzerland, near Basel. This concrete Goetheanum had replaced a more elaborate double-domed wooden one that had burned down on New Year's Eve 1922–23. The story of Fire in the Temple comes from what I learned during that summer of '81, as well as from many years—nearly four decades now—of subsequent conversations, study, research, and experiences. The specific idea of this play—chosen from among several possible projects—was conceived in September 2017, on a camping trip in Maine. Focused research and a quest through stacks of books followed, then numerous—both informal and semi-staged—readings, crucial input from dramaturgs and friends, countless rewrites and revisions, and a full production in September 2023. This script is the result.

It is a history play about a group of people in Switzerland between the World Wars, a time of tremendous tensions and world-shaping decisions. I have tried to let these people speak for themselves and to reveal their inner experiences and their worldview. The play focuses on the last 27 months of Rudolf Steiner's life—his relationships and deeds and the events surrounding them. Most of the words of the characters, especially of Steiner himself, are their own, translated from the German and edited and adapted for the theater.

Glen Williamson
September, 2018
New York City
revised April 2021 and August 2024

A Note from the Playwright

Fire in the Temple is based on selected documents (lectures, letters, memoirs, and personal notes and anecdotes) from the time-span of the play (1922–1925). Most of the dialogue is drawn from actual words of the historic persons involved—often with only minimal adaptation or retranslation. However, I have taken some artistic license when necessary, while—I hope—remaining faithful to the historic events and characters.

Setting

The action takes place in Dornach, Switzerland, and in other locations in Europe, throughout 1923, 1924, and early 1925, with flashbacks to ancient and medieval times.

CHARACTERS

RUDOLF STEINER / CRATYLUS / ARISTOTLE / THOMAS
AQUINAS

ITA WEGMAN / MYSA / ALEXANDER / REGINALD

MARIE STEINER / THEOPHRASTUS / ALBERTUS

FRÄULEIN SAMWALLER, "SAM"

MISS EDITH MARYON

EHRENFRIED PFEIFFER

GÜNTHER WACHSMUTH

ELISABETH VREEDE

THE GRAND MASTER OF A SECRET ORDER

A BROTHER OF THE SECRET ORDER

THE ARCHANGEL MICHAÉL (EURYTHMIST[*])

ADDITIONAL ROLES COVERED BY PERFORMERS
PLAYING THE ABOVE

WHISPERING AUDIENCE MEMBERS

A BROWNSHIRT

VOICE OF MICHAÉL

(THE SCULPTURE)

GREEN DEMONS

KLINGSOR

---

[*]   Eurythmy is an art of movement, integral to this story.

Note on Casting and Staging

Fire in the Temple can be performed by a cast of ten actors (five women, five men), plus the eurythmist playing Michaél, and a musician. The actress playing Sam should also be a skilled eurythmist or will need a eurythmist double. The Green Demons may be depicted in movement by additional eurythmists and/or by the actors who play Sam, Ehrenfried, Miss Maryon, and Elisabeth Vreede.

The single stage set may indicate the carpentry shop. In the premiere production, it was a sculpted wall with a doorway and two platforms, one on either side, with steps. Railed stairs lead offstage. One platform can become a bed. The action is continuous. Chairs and props come and go, as scene changes are effected by lighting, costume, music, and the ensemble.

Stage directions are suggestions—from the playwright or from the director of the original production—and need not be strictly followed.

Music: A cello plays various motifs, and embellishes scene changes.

Rudolf Steiner "Dr. Steiner" or "Herr Doctor" (*age 61*)
Austrian-born philosopher, scientist, social reformer, educator, architect, and clairvoyant spiritual researcher. Prolific lecturer, author, and teacher. Hungarian looks, with a fiery glow and hair blacker than coal. Medium stature, slim build, remarkable eyes—kind and full of goodwill. Unaffectedly elegant and likable. Often wears a well-worn black suit with a long-tailed coat, his tie a soft, loosely knotted piece of black silk with flowing ends. Very upright yet fluid posture, even when tired, burdened, or ill; head back and tilted slightly forward. Eyes like an eagle, but full of infinite pain, never-ending love, and warmth. Energetic and active, but always from a state of calm, restful ease—even in the midst of great stress and activity. Astonishing memory. Light, certain step, which can become heavy at times. Still, quiet head. Agile hands. A most *human* human being. Different from anyone else, but not eccentric in any way. Sociable, amicable, and gallantly humorous; able to laugh heartily in spite of his deeply serious nature. Capable of rapid transformation and selfless flexibility. A citizen of two worlds, simultaneously on earth and in the heavens. Also appears as Cratylus, Aristotle, and Thomas Aquinas.

Marie Steiner (von Sivers) "Frau Doctor" or "Frau Steiner" (*age 55*) Wife and close colleague of Rudolf Steiner. Actress and elocutionist devoted to purely artistic speaking and to the new movement art of eurythmy. Born in Russia of German nobility. Full of warmth and life, but outspoken, critical, and uncompromising. With a mighty voice, she can speak with childlike directness, great earnestness or rage, laugh heartily, or heartily rebel. Behind her self-control, which can some-

times seem to be a cool pride, glows the fire of a genuine
volcano. Under the ice, her eyes can flicker with rage or with
love. Wakeful, well prepared, and well organized. Once light
and graceful, she is now mostly bound to her wheelchair. Also
appears as Theophrastus and Albertus.

ITA WEGMAN (*age 46*) Pupil and, later, close colleague of Rudolf Steiner. Medical doctor and practicing physician at her
own clinic. A strong-willed, deeply sensitive Dutch woman,
born in Indonesia. Wise but not intellectual. Warmheart-
ed, fearless, and matter-of-fact. Definite yet springing step,
bright beaming eyes. Also appears as Mysa, Alexander, and
Reginald.

FRÄULEIN SAMWALLER, "SAM" (*age 38*) Friend, pupil, and co-
worker of Rudolf and Marie Steiner in Dornach and Berlin.
Eurythmist. Often assists Marie Steiner in various ways. In-
tuitive, direct, and unabashed. (Somewhat fictional, based
closely on several historic persons, especially Anna Samweber
and Mieta Waller, but also Ilona Schubert, Margarita Woloschin, Maria Röschl, Marie Savitch, and Louise Clason.)

GÜNTHER WACHSMUTH (*age 29*) German lawyer and economist. Administrator. A young man with a purpose, he speaks
quickly and matter-of-factly, but is sometimes impulsive. (In
this play, the character of Günther Wachsmuth also encompasses aspects of his brother Wolfgang and of Albert Steffen,
the renowned Swiss poet and dramatist.)

ELISABETH VREEDE (*age 43*) Dutch mathematician and astron-
omer. Strong, quiet presence, but often overlooked. Well
dressed, simply and tastefully. Hair parted in the middle and
pulled back. Walks and stands calmly, resting within herself.
Speaks little, but with unrelenting simplicity and truthfulness.

EHRENFRIED PFEIFFER (*age 23*) Pupil and coworker of Rudolf
Steiner. German student of physics and biochemistry, a soil

scientist and stage-lighting designer and technician. Serious and devoted, though also energetic and outspoken.

MISS (EDITH) MARYON (*age 50*) English sculptress and close and unstinting collaborator with Rudolf Steiner on their massive wooden sculpture and on the Goetheanum building. Profoundly sensitive in body and soul, she has a chronic lung disease. Voluminous hair, which she wears piled up in a loosely sculpted coif.

THE ARCHANGEL MICHAÉL (*ageless*) Appears as a spiritual being and moves with majestic gestures of the art of eurythmy. (Should be played by a master eurythmist, his lines usually spoken by an offstage speaker's voice.) He may also appear as the striding figure of the sculpture.

THE GRAND MASTER (*age 70s*) Leader of a lodge of a secret order that opposes Rudolf Steiner's work. (Somewhat fictional, based on [an inversion of] the character Hilary Gottgetreu in Steiner's mystery dramas.) May wear ritual robes or business clothes.

SECRET BROTHER (*younger than the Grand Master*) A member of the secret order and protégé of the Grand Master. Somewhat ambivalent about opposing Dr. Steiner. (Based on a later acquaintance of Ehrenfried Pfeiffer.) Wears inconspicuous business suit.

GREEN DEMONS (*ageless and primeval*) Snakelike reptilian demonic beings who move silently and menacingly. May be played by eurythmists, dancers, or mimes, or depicted with puppets, smoke, or projected lights. However these demons are portrayed, they should be visible just enough to be subtly but seriously ominous. In the original production, they each wore a green cape and hood and a single, slithering, wormlike white glove.

KLINGSOR (*ageless and agèd*) Evil sorcerer. Can be played by the eurythmist who plays Michaél.

Fire in the Temple has been in development since September 2017. A full-cast premiere production, directed by John McManus, was presented in Copake and Spring Valley, NY, and Kimberton, PA, in September 2023, with the following cast and production team:

ARCHANGEL MICHAÉL — Zachary Dolphin

RUDOLF STEINER — Peter Josephson

MARIE STEINER — Laurie Portocarrero

ITA WEGMAN — Rosibel Mejia

FRÄULEIN SAMWALLER, "SAM" — Kayla Hope Nicosia

EDITH MARYON — Faith DiVecchio

EHRENFRIED PFEIFFER — Liam McGilligan

GÜNTHER WACHSMUTH — Dhruva Corrigan

ELISABETH VREEDE — Catherine Decker

GRAND MASTER — Vincent Roppolo

SECRET BROTHER — Marke Levene

EURYTHMIST SAM — Sea-Anna Vasilas, Victoria Sander

KLINGSOR — Zachary Dolphin

VOICE OF MICHAÉL — Marke Levene

GREEN DEMONS — Victoria Sander, Sea-Anna Vasilas, Kayla Hope Nicosia, Faith DiVecchio, Catherine Decker, Liam McGilligan

CELLO — Nathaniel Drake

GONGS, CHIMES, AND SOUND EFFECTS
Berenika Lehrman

Director — John McManus

Set Design — Gary Osborne

Costume Design — Peggy Walsh

Lighting Design — Deena Pewtherer

Original Music — Nathaniel Drake

Stage Manager — Henry DiVecchio

Production Manager — Patrick Doyle

Executive Producer and General Manager

Glen Williamson

Assistant Lighting Designer

Patrick Doyle

Set Construction — Nathaniel Blachere

Props, Sound, and Light Crew — Berenika Lehrman

Lighting for touring performances — Ethan Sudan

Eurythmy Choreography — Sea-Anna Vasilas, Zachary
Dolphin, John McManus, Victoria Sander

Additional Costumes — Berenika Lehrman, Zachary
Dolphin, Sea-Anna Vasilas, Eurythmy Spring Valley

As of July 2024, full-cast staged readings have also been presented by companies in England and South Africa; two-person staged readings continue to tour; and further full-scale productions are being considered.

Act 1

Scene 1: The Work

A large concert hall, May 1922. GÜNTHER WACHSMUTH *addresses the audience as people are still settling.*

WACHSMUTH   Ladies and gentlemen, please find your seats. If you are standing, keep the aisles clear. Two thousand people now are crowding in here. Thank you for being patient. Rudolf Steiner, the famous spiritual scientist and founder of the Waldorf school, will be addressing you in just a moment. Despite the obstacles, we will proceed.

WHISPERINGS IN THE AUDIENCE
(1) I've been anticipating this for months. (2) They say his lectures earlier this year attracted more than twenty thousand people. (3) He spoke in every major German city.

(A burst of applause as DR. STEINER *enters.* WACHSMUTH *and* EHRENFRIED *stand by.)*

DR. STEINER   Our civilization is in need of healing. Grave problems are confronting us today. And here in Central Europe we can look for solutions that have not yet been considered: Three separate realms of life must be developed to guide a healthy social organism—freedom in culture and religion; equality in politics and rights; and brotherhood in economic dealings.

(*A brownshirt wearing a swastika [the actor who plays the* Secret Brother] *yells from the back of the audience.*)

Brownshirt
You're an enemy of the German people, corrupting the Fatherland. (*storming the stage*) False prophet, polluting our nation. You traitor!

(*Demonic music rises as shadowy, dragonlike* Green Demons *flood the stage.* Wachsmuth *and* Ehrenfried *escort* Dr. Steiner *to safety. Chaos. Blackout.*)

Dr. Steiner
(*in the darkness*) O Guardian of Heaven, Archangel Michaél!

(*The* Archangel Michaél *appears as a eurythmist in radiant light.*)

Michaél
(*speaking*) What do you seek?

Dr. Steiner
(*now visible*) I want to kindle every human being to become a flame, shining its fiery essence from within—to cultivate a science of the spirit, exploring what lies beyond material knowledge, to bring new life to thinking that is dead.

Michaél
Success of your expansive spirit task needs human understanding on the earth to overcome the dragon's threat'ning power.

(*Music.* Michaél *confronts the dragon [the* Green Demons], *then disappears. Lights shift.*)

Dr. Steiner
(*now intimately addressing his pupils, the audience*) Dear friends, the path of spirit knowledge

starts within you. Within each human being slumber faculties through which we can acquire for ourselves knowledge of higher worlds. If we develop—deep within ourselves—forces that are still slumbering there, we can perceive a world of soul and spirit as real for us as what we see and touch physically with our eyes and with our hands.

(*The* Grand Master *of the dark lodge of a secret brotherhood appears on a platform, wearing ritual robes.* Green Demons *are present.*)

Grand Master   This teacher Rudolf Steiner must be stopped. His teachings are diminishing the power of our secret brotherhood.

Dr. Steiner   (*continuing to the audience*) This knowledge shouldn't be accumulated to be a pers'nal treasure for oneself, but to be placed in service of the world. The world needs this spirit knowledge—actively working in all fields of life. In science, medicine, and economics, in education and in all the arts.

Grand Master   (*to the now-visible* Secret Brother) He knows the truth about our secret knowledge, revealing it to everyone in his "Anthroposophical Society"—to *women*, even—and he's founding independent schools for children, freeing their thinking. We don't want new ideas!

Dr. Steiner   (*now in the audience, in front of the stage*) Dear boys and girls of the Waldorf School. Today you are beginning a new grade. In life, you see, we're always getting older. And you will find some people with gray hair. Whenever they see children, they think, "What would I be now without my teachers, who guided me along in my school days?" That is why my heart is filled with joy when you tell me how much you love your teachers. But nothing can be done without hard work. If you work hard, then what you learn by loving your teachers will become real strength for you. And you will grow up to be good and capable people working in the world.

(GÜNTHER WACHSMUTH, *holding a shovel, joins* DR. STEINER. *Summer. A farm in Germany.*)

GRAND MASTER He uses his clairvoyant faculties to research hidden truths and freely shares them. He's even giving his advice to farmers.

(DR. STEINER *addresses a group of farmers (another part of the audience).* ELISABETH VREEDE *is now visible, listening.*)

DR. STEINER Why is it no longer possible to find potatoes as good as the ones I ate when I was a boy? That's a simple fact; I've tried it everywhere. You can't even find such potatoes in the countryside where I ate them then. Nutritional value has especially declined in recent decades. The delicate influences from the universe at work within the soil are no longer understood by farmers—except perhaps by some of you who've hung on instinctively to bits of the old knowledge. Most farmers don't know what goes on in the soil in their own fields. They are astonished when they get big potatoes or other vegetables that swell and grow large in size. But when these vegetables are consumed, they do little more than fill the stomach. Present-day sciences and chemistry are incapable of nourishing the human organism—they simply don't find the right way to go about it. The insights of *spiritual* science must be put into practice by the middle of this century, or unspeakable harm will be done to the land, to nature, and to human health. (*taking the shovel*) For example, I will show you how to mix and apply manure preparations, which should be brought to the widest possible acreage throughout the globe.

(WACHSMUTH [*with the shovel*] *and* ELISABETH VREEDE *exit.*)

GRAND MASTER   And now, in Switzerland, he's built a temple exposing and expounding sacred teachings; calls it the "Goetheanum;" and it's crafted . . . completely out of wood.

DR. STEINER   (*stepping farther into the audience, up the aisle*) Please come in from the stairs and antechamber. This is our large-dome auditorium. You see the stage there in the smaller dome. I have attempted to design this building in an entirely organic way—each detail in its place within the whole. Just think about the shape of your earlobe: a small part of your body, but you can't imagine such a shape is suitable for growing on the top of your big toe. Each of these wooden columns, for example—the murals there and all the colored windows—grew from their place within the architecture and can't be separated from the whole. And every word that's uttered from this stage must speak the truth expressed in the whole building, just as the nose on your face reveals, through its form, the truth of your whole being.

GRAND MASTER He seems to think, dear brother, that the time has come to open up the doors of knowledge to ordinary people, without protection of our sacred rites.

SECRET BROTHER Exalted Master, I have vowed, as you have, by our sacred oath of brotherhood, to protect our secrets. But is it really necessary to so forcefully condemn this Rudolf Steiner?

GRAND MASTER He's brought our condemnation on himself.

SCENE 2: THE FIRE

*Coughing in the audience. Fire horns. Smoke. New Year's Eve, 1922.
Miss Maryon enters through the audience with Dr. Ita Wegman, coming
out of the smoke-filled building.*

MISS MARYON	(*coughing*) Oh Dr. Wegman, this is dreadful!
ITA	(*handing her a cloth*) Miss Maryon. Hold this over your mouth and nose. And breathe. Physicians! Are there any other physicians here?!
MISS MARYON	Dr. Steiner (*she coughs*), he. . . (*she coughs more.*)
ITA	Now breathe, Miss Maryon.
MISS MARYON	He is risking his life! (*she coughs even more.*)
ITA	Yes. But there is nothing more you can do right now. Just breathe!
	(ITA *sits with her.*)
DR. STEINER	(*coming out, also gasping for air*) Is anyone still inside? Wachsmuth!
WACHSMUTH	(*coming out of the building, coughing*) I'm right here.
DR. STEINER	Breathing the smoke is deadly.
WACHSMUTH	It's getting denser. It's filling the whole auditorium.
DR. STEINER	Where is Ita Wegman? Dr. Wegman!

ITA

I'm here with Miss Maryon.

DR. STEINER

Ah, good. And Fräulein Samwaller?

WACHSMUTH

She's salvaging the costumes.

DR. STEINER

She has to come out immediately. Sam!

(*He goes back in.*)

WACHSMUTH

Dr. Steiner, don't go back in! (*he looks around*) Herr Steffen! Where is Albert Steffen? (*he steps offstage.*)

(ELISABETH VREEDE *steps onto the stage, holding a cloth over her mouth. She has a strong, quiet presence, but no one seems to notice her.* FRÄULEIN SAMWALLER [*"*SAM*"*] *hurries down the aisle carrying costumes.*)

SAM

(*coughing*) I saved these costumes! But flames have broken through the murals in the large dome and above the stage.

DR. STEINER

(*coming out after* SAM) Who else is not accounted for?

WACHSMUTH

(*stepping back onstage*) Herr Steffen is here. He's just catching his breath.

DR. STEINER

Good. Ehrenfried Pfeiffer! Wachsmuth, where is Herr Pfeiffer?

OTHERS

(*overlapping with the following*) Herr Pfeiffer! Where is he? Ehrenfried Pfeiffer?

WACHSMUTH

He must still be inside.

SAM

He's checking the electric wiring.

DR. STEINER

I'll look.

(He goes back in.)

SAM

No, Herr Doctor, it's too late.

ITA

I hope he hasn't passed out inside!

(The fire horns get louder. Suddenly EHRENFRIED *emerges, exhausted, followed by* DR. STEINER*.)*

EHRENFRIED

(coughing and gasping for breath) The carved-glass windows are bursting.

DR. STEINER

Ehrenfried, is anyone still in there?

EHRENFRIED

No. I'm the last.

WACHSMUTH

Where is Frau Doctor Steiner?!

DR. STEINER

She is safe at home in House Hansi. Is Elisabeth Vreede here?

ELISABETH VREEDE

Yes. I'm here.

WACHSMUTH

Oh! Fräulein Vreede. I didn't even see you there!

SAM

Look. More fire hoses are coming.

EHRENFRIED

It's too late. The blaze is engulfing the entire Goetheanum.

WACHSMUTH

It can't be saved!

(The fire horns stop. Everyone turns to DR. STEINER*.)*

DR. STEINER   There is nothing we can do. We have to abandon the Goetheanum and save the carpentry shop. *(he steps downstage.)*

EHRENFRIED   And the studio. *(he hurries off, up the steps.)*

WACHSMUTH   Save the sculpture! It's Miss Maryon and Dr. Steiner's masterpiece!

(He exits after EHRENFRIED.*)*

SAM   Look! Flames are bursting through the roof. I've never seen anything like it.

ITA   Oh, this is shattering.

MISS MARYON   It's a nightmare.

(Bells in the distance.)

SAM   It's midnight. The New Year!

ELISABETH VREEDE

(contemplatively, unheard by the others) 1923.

(The lights change. SAM *picks up the costumes and exits up the stairs.* ITA WEGMAN *stands alone upstage.)*

ITA   *(quietly, to herself)* In one night. Utterly destroyed. Such unspeakable sadness.

*(*DR. STEINER *stands downstage, alone among the ruins, gazing into the glowing flames.)*

DR. STEINER   The Goetheanum's forms and images could have wakened ancient memories—and an awareness of Michaél.

ITA — (*approaching, barely able to speak*) This is terrible for us.

DR. STEINER — Yes, Frau Doctor Wegman. The Goetheanum was a call from the spirit world, but no hearts responded. Now everything has been inscribed in the cosmic memory: the possibility and the silence. Only jealousy did not stay mute.

ITA — Dr. Steiner, my heart longs for your work to go forward. I've been working on my own all these years. But from now on, I will be there completely for you and for our work.

(MICHAËL *appears.*)

MICHAËL — (*speaking himself*) Remember your faithful companion (*offstage voice for eurythmy*) in ancient and faraway lifetimes.

DR. STEINER — Will she remember? She has the will to heal people; and she knows exactly how to distinguish the gods' working through me from what is *human* in me. But she doesn't remember our friendship through many earthly lives. (MICHAËL *gestures.*) The spirit world would rejoice if she would remember.

(*Music. Gongs. Lights shift. Circular movement. With simple costume accessories brought to them,* ITA *becomes* YOUNG ALEXANDER *and* DR. STEINER *becomes* ARISTOTLE.)

ALEXANDER (ITA) — Why did the Temple of Artemis have to burn? Tell me, my teacher Aristotle?

Aristotle (Dr. Steiner)

> O Alexander, you are young and full of questions. But I am old and weary of the world.

Alexander

> You *brought* me to this distant island, Samothrace. Can I learn here about the fire in Ephesus?

Aristotle

> This island's altars still resound with cosmic wisdom.

Alexander

> My mother said the Temple burned when I was born.

Aristotle

> Yes, Artemis became a midwife at your birth.

Alexander

> The Goddess Artemis was there in Macedonia?!

Aristotle:

> She left her temple back in Ephesus unguarded; and jealous gods allowed a man to light the fire.

Alexander

> But why? What is the meaning of this for my future?

Aristotle

> This tragic memory inspires a cosmic script. The secrets of the world, of matter and of spirit, are written there. Be still, and read your destiny.

Alexander

> (*inwardly reading the cosmic script*) Oh. . . I read that I must go into the East. Yes, I wish to walk upon the fiery earth! I will rebuild the Temple of the Goddess. And I will bring your teachings everywhere I go.

Aristotle

> Go, Alexander. Conquer the world.

> (Alexander *exits*.)

My heart goes with you.

(*Music. Lights shift. Circular movement. He becomes* Dr. Steiner *again.* Michaél *gestures.*)

MICHAÉL   (*with offstage voice*) Behold the cosmic Word within the scorching fire, and find the answer in the shrine of Artemis.

DR. STEINER   The jealousy of gods.

(*Music.* Michaél *disappears.* Ita, Wachsmuth, Ehrenfried, Miss Maryon, Elisabeth Vreede, *and* Sam *reappear at the smoldering ruins.*)

The jealousy of man.

(*He takes a step and nearly falls.* Miss Maryon *catches him.*)

ITA   Dr. Steiner!

DR. STEINER   Thank you, Miss Maryon.

MISS MARYON   Come. (*helping him sit*) You can rest here.

(Sam *runs up the stairs.*)

WACHSMUTH   Fräulein Samwaller, what are you doing?

EHRENFRIED   She's sliding down the stair rail.

(*She does.*)

WACHSMUTH   (*to* Sam) Are you crazy?

SAM   No, Herr Wachsmuth. It's the *New Year*!!

(*She runs up the stairs again.*)

EHRENFRIED   She's lost her mind.

WACHSMUTH   She's gone insane.

(*She slides down again.*)

DR. STEINER   She is the most sane person here.

(MARIE, *in her wheelchair, alone in Haus Hansi, waiting anxiously.*)

MARIE   Smoke in the hallway!? — That's all they said, and it's been hours. What is happening up there?! Oh, if only I could have walked back up there with him. But he begged me to stay home. And I would be useless like this anyway. Oh, why are these *legs so painful*?! To think, I was an *actress*—and now I am lame. But I should be there by his side, whatever is happening. (*turning her wheelchair*) Meyer! Herr Meyer, are you there?! Can you drive me back up the hill? (*she exits.*)

(*The scene continues, now as if indoors.* DR. STEINER *is still sitting.* WACHSMUTH *and* EHRENFRIED *have gone.*)

MISS MARYON   (*exhausted, nearly in tears*) They've dragged our sculpture out into the open. The sculpture that you and I are still carving! I can't bear it. Our magnificent striding figure of Christ is standing in pieces out in the snow.

DR. STEINER   They shouldn't have done that without asking me.

MISS MARYON   It should have been our building's crowning glory.

DR. STEINER   We will move it back inside in the morning.

MISS MARYON   In the morning.

DR. STEINER   So much work, all destroyed. Ten years of devoted sacrifice by friends from many nations.

MISS MARYON   I will never recover from this.

DR. STEINER   Nor will I—

(EHRENFRIED *enters holding a cup of tea.*)

EHRENFRIED   I've brought some tea.

MISS MARYON   Oh, don't disturb him. He's . . .

DR. STEINER   Miss Maryon, let him come, if he wants to be so kind.

(*She exits.* EHRENFRIED *crosses to him.* DR. STEINER *does not move.* SAM *sits at a distance.*)

DR. STEINER   Sit with me, Ehrenfried.

(EHRENFRIED *sits near* DR. STEINER *and sets down the tea between them. Lights shift.*)

My strength is depleted.

EHRENFRIED   Dr. Steiner, I'll give you all *my* strength. Oh, "What ails thee, Uncle?" That's the question Parsifal asked the wounded Grail King.

(*Lights shift. Music.* KLINGSOR *appears.*)

EHRENFRIED   Klingsor, the evil sorcerer, had wounded him and the wound would not heal until someone asked.

DR. STEINER   Yes. And now Klingsor and his hordes of demons are lurking close.

EHRENFRIED: Is Klingsor real?

DR. STEINER   Oh yes, and he bears goodwill toward no one. The dragon—yes, truly—a terrible dragon is threatening us.

EHRENFRIED: The Archangel Michaél conquers the dragon.

DR. STEINER   Yes. But only if people wake up to him.

(DR. STEINER, *at last, picks up the tea and drinks.* WACHSMUTH *and* ITA *enter.*)

ITA   Have you been able to rest?

DR. STEINER   We have battled with demons.

SAM   (*standing*) Oh, Herr Doctor—

DR. STEINER   Sam, please go to Frau Steiner in Haus Hansi and stay with her. Tell her I will come down again soon. You know, Sam, she will have very hard times. You will stand by her, won't you, Sam?

SAM   Yes, Herr Doctor, I will.

(SAM *exits.* WACHSMUTH *begins to exit.*)

EHRENFRIED   (*realizing* ITA *is waiting for him to leave*) I'll go and look after the carpentry shop.

WACHSMUTH   The carpentry shop is practically under water. The walls still feel hot. And everything is covered in soot.

(WACHSMUTH *and* EHRENFRIED *exit.*)

ITA   This is devastating for all of the members. What will now become of the Anthroposophical Society?

DR. STEINER   The smoking embers show the Society's *inner* state, which lies in ruins. (*pointing*) There is the place where the arsonist was able to make the hole! Come. We must go on. In spiritual work, there is no failure, only diversion and delay. We will build again. Let's put the carpentry shop back in order. (*he exits with* ITA)

Scene 3: Pain

Marie *enters in her wheelchair, with* Sam.

MARIE All I could see from the window was a reddish glow in the sky. How could this have happened?!

SAM They say the fire must've been smoldering inside the walls during the lecture, even during your performance.

MARIE It's not possible! After the lecture—even in this wheelchair—I felt blessed and joyfully uplifted. The moonlit night, stars glistening in the heavens. I could see the gods rejoicing—exulting at our magical wooden temple, our glorious Goetheanum! And now it's gone?!

SAM Yes, it's gone.

MARIE Ten years of loving craftsmanship. Like the building of Solomon's Temple. Every inch hand-carved.

SAM Oh, Frau Doctor, I knew.

MARIE Our stage! Our podium! Our Temple of the Word! It was a revelation of the sacred Mysteries.

SAM It was a horrendous fire, just at midnight, just as the bells were ringing in the new year—it was a sight to behold: there were colors in the

	flames from the melting organ pipes, and the columns became torches . . .
MARIE	Stop! Say no more. Seeing it would have killed me.

(*Music.* Dr. Steiner *brings* Sam *her eurythmy costume and* Marie *her text.* Wachsmuth, Ehrenfried, Ita, *and* Elisabeth Vreede *sit, their backs to the audience, as Sam goes off to prepare.* Miss Maryon *sits to one side, extremely weak. With* Dr. Steiner's *help, Marie stands up, courageously suppressing her own feelings and the pain in her legs.* Dr. Steiner *steps onto a platform.*)

DR. STEINER	(*addressing the audience*) My dear friends: We are continuing, here in the carpentry shop, the lectures and artistic performances we would have held in our auditorium. Frau Doctor Steiner has graciously agreed to recite for us—and Fräulein Samwaller will make visible in our new art of *eurythmy*—a remarkably prophetic poem written nearly thirty years ago.
MARIE	"Fire in the Temple" (*she pauses to overcome her emotions.*) "Знамение" [ZnamEHnye], by Vladimir Solovyov:

(Sam *enters to perform eurythmy.* Marie *recites eloquently.*)

MARIE
Even though in the sleeping temple
there is a hellish glow amid the darkness
and thunder in the silence,

though everything around us lies in ruins,
the banner will not waver, and the shield
will not move from the crumbled wall.

In horror, half-awake, we came
running to see the holy place,
our temple filled with stifling fumes
and melted chunks of silver strewn about.
Black smoke clung to the charred and tattered carpets.

But heavenly light shone
on the serpent's futile poison,
and the imperishable covenant
stood as before between the earth and heaven.

> (*The eurythmist,* Sam, *exits.* Marie *and* Dr. Stein-
> er *look at each other across the stage.*)

> (*The four pupils begin to leave.*)

Dr. Steiner   When the Great War ended, people were happy and relieved. They didn't realize the magnitude of the upheavals yet to come. But sleeping souls will have a rude awakening one day; they'll rub their eyes and drop their sleeping caps, when the catastrophe continues on its course.

> (*The others exit through the doorway. Haus Hansi.*)

Marie   I'm worried about you.

> (Dr. Steiner *helps her sit down in her wheelchair. The lights shift.*)

Marie   The destruction is heart-crushing.

DR. STEINER Oh, dear Marie, if you're always worried about me, then I have to worry about your worrying.

MARIE A life's work, devastated!

DR. STEINER You are so dear to me. Surely all will be well with both of us.

MARIE So long as our destiny continues to allow us to live and work together.

DR. STEINER Yes, I feel truly fortunate that you are a companion in my work. Deep within your soul, you cultivate artistic feeling without a trace of sentimentality.

MARIE And you continue to do the impossible. You are still traveling more than the queen of Sheba!

DR. STEINER I couldn't do any of it without you.

MARIE Oh, dear Heart, you are too gracious.

DR. STEINER But my dear Mouse, *I* only have to write—and speak as a guest lecturer. But *you* have organized the whole Anthroposophical Society, with thousands of members and friends. You carry a godly power in your soul.

MARIE And I am also your cleaning lady.

DR. STEINER (*smiling*) You do clean up difficulties in ways that I can't. And our movement could only be founded—with all that we built up, in Berlin—because you asked if it would be possible. In accordance with spiritual laws, I could then take action. I no longer had to remain silent, because you, my dear, had *asked the question.*

MARIE

And I have been by your side ever since—and always will be.

DR. STEINER

We've been together in many incarnations.

MARIE

Yes. I do feel that . . .

DR. STEINER

Last time you were *my* teacher. Do you remember?

MARIE

Only vaguely. I long ago realized who *you* were then.—But why am I suffering with this lameness now?

DR. STEINER

It's not a punishment. Your suffering comes with your capacity for sacrifice and selfless work.

MARIE

Why must my creative spirit transform into its opposite?

DR. STEINER

A cosmic being works within you, and her creative force can cause you pain, in order to sow seeds for future growth.

(*Music.* MICHAÉL *appears in radiant light around* MARIE. *She exits.*)

Scene 4: Loss

The lights shift. Michaél *gestures his ritual.*

DR. STEINER O Archangel Michaél, so much has been forgotten on the earth. The spirits of the sun illumined millions of your pupils in centuries past, in your school in spirit realms. Now they are asleep. And the dragon is awake.

(*Demon music.* Michaél *exits.* Dr. Steiner *crosses to* Ehrenfried, *who brings him tea.*)

(*Lights shift, revealing split scene. The lodge of the Secret Brotherhood. The* Grand Master, *with the* Secret Brother. Green Demons *are present.*)

SECRET BROTHER But, Exalted Master, the destruction of his temple seems to have emboldened him.

GRAND MASTER This fire ignited by our allies of the Church failed to stop him or to end his work, but his life forces have been damaged, and also his physical health.

SECRET BROTHER What do you mean, "our allies of the Church"?! The Roman Church has been our enemy for centuries.

GRAND MASTER In this we're in agreement with the Church. Rudolf Steiner is a threat to them as well.

(Ehrenfried *and* Dr. Steiner *in quiet conversation.*)

DR. STEINER   When I was a little boy, I liked to play in the waiting room of my father's train station. One day I was sitting on a bench there, and a woman came in whom I had never seen before, although she had a strong family resemblance to my mother. She reached out to me with heart-wrenching gestures, begging me to do anything I could for her, now and in the future. Then she disappeared into the stove in the corner. And in the flames of the stove, I could see images of what had led to the woman's death. I was deeply troubled and perplexed by this. But there was no one I could speak to about it. Years later, I learned that, in that very hour, my mother's sister, who lived far away, had killed herself. I had, without a doubt, seen the spirit of my aunt, asking me for help after she had died. And from that moment on, I knew how to live more intimately in spirit worlds. Nature spirits and creative beings were just as real to me as impressions of the outer world.

EHRENFRIED   So, you knew before anyone else that your aunt had died?

DR. STEINER   When I tried to tell my parents, they didn't believe me. My jovial father only said, "Don't be a silly boy."

(*Lights shift.*)

SECRET BROTHER   But he's just a peasant from a family in Hungary. His father was a station master for the Railroad. And now they call him "Dr. Steiner." He's no *doctor*.

GRAND MASTER   He's a doctor of *philosophy*. He studied in Vienna and edited the scientific works of Goethe. So don't underestimate him. He has a massive following in Germany, and now he's lecturing all over Europe. You fail to understand: There are destructive forces hidden deep within each human soul; and for the sake of all *humanity*, our knowledge of these forces must be guarded. We cannot allow him to continue.

(*Lights shift.*)

EHRENFRIED   And did you also know that the Goetheanum would burn?

DR. STEINER   Yes, Ehrenfried, I knew. When I first visited this hill ten years ago, during the night I saw it all: Everything would be destroyed. Not a single stick would still remain.

EHRENFRIED   And yet you resolved to go ahead and build it. Why?

DR. STEINER   I knew that higher knowledge could begin to grow in anyone who entered there. It would be a temple for the flaming thirst for knowledge that can rise up in every human heart.

ALEXANDER (ITA)   (*loudly, off stage*) But Aristotle, . . .

(*Gong.* DR. STEINER *hears, hands* EHRENFRIED *his teacup.*)

DR. STEINER   Thank you, Ehrenfried.

EHRENFRIED   Thank *you*, Doctor Steiner.

(EHRENFRIED *exits. Music. Circular Movement. Gong. Finger chimes.* MARIE *enters as* THEOPHRASTUS; ITA, *as* ALEXANDER. DR. STEINER *becomes* ARISTOTLE.)

ALEXANDER

. . .what is left, then, to distinguish us—who are well schooled in what you teach—from all the others, if *everyone* now partakes of these high teachings? Do you do right to circulate them?

ARISTOTLE (DR. STEINER)

Is it your view, Alexander, that they should be kept secret? You see, I have made them public, yet I have *not* made them public. For only those who have heard me can comprehend them.

ALEXANDER

(*agreeing*) The privilege to comprehend your knowledge of the Mysteries is of more value to me than all my kingly power.

ARISTOTLE

Remain healthy, O King Alexander!

ALEXANDER

May you remain well, my teacher!

(ALEXANDER *exjts. Music. Gong.*)

THEOPHRASTUS (MARIE)

But Aristotle, that drunken boy, Alexander, understands nothing of your teachings. He is incapable and *infertile*. They say his semen's watery from excessive drink.

ARISTOTLE

My faithful Theophrastus. You lack your godly voice. He has his task, and you have yours.

THEOPHRASTUS   Yes, my teacher Aristotle. Whatever *he* may accomplish, *I* will be the one to preserve your teachings for the times to come.

(*Music. Gong.* THEOPHRASTUS *exits.* ARISTOTLE *becomes* DR. STEINER *again.*)

Scene 5: Help

Outside the Goetheanum ruins, Wachsmuth *and* Sam *enter from different directions, each with newspapers.*

WACHSMUTH   Dr. St. . .

SAM   (*simultaneously*) Herr Doctor. . .

WACHSMUTH   (*to* Sam) Excuse me. (*turning to* Dr. Steiner *and continuing as* Sam *sits down to wait*) These newspapers dare to proclaim that you should have foreseen this disastrous fire and prevented it, since you are clairvoyant.

DR. STEINER   When one serves the spirit world as I do, one may not use one's clairvoyant faculties to protect oneself, even if it means one's life's work is destroyed.

WACHSMUTH   But how can *we* protect you from these vicious condemnations and attacks?

DR. STEINER   Doctor Wachsmuth, the press has been making a caricature of our work for years.

WACHSMUTH   But now they are positively wallowing in this stupidity.

DR. STEINER   (*perusing an article*) It is pure venom to print this after the fact. Jealousy—and a fear of waking up to the spirit.

WACHSMUTH   Dr. Steiner, how can our movement survive?

Religious fanatics are using every conceivable weapon against you. And the National Socialists have denounced you as a threat to the German state. Our work has powerful opponents and they are growing stronger and stronger.

DR. STEINER   No matter how strong these opponents may be, our own positive energy must be equally strong.

WACHSMUTH   Then tell me, is there something we can do in meditation to defend you—and the Society— from such attacks?

DR. STEINER   (*after reflection*) If you can bring together a group of people who have that question, I will show you how to begin.—It would be good if you would speak with Dr. Wegman.

WACHSMUTH   Dr. Wegman? But it's so difficult to reason with her. Her first language is Dutch, and she doesn't know how to think.

DR. STEINER   Wachsmuth, please. We shouldn't be surprised to meet such monstrous *outer* opposition when we have *internal* opposition.

WACHSMUTH   Yes, Herr Doctor. But my brother and I and several others wish to help after the fire, to offer our united strength to you.

DR. STEINER   Help has already come to me from the spirit world! You each have your meditation exercises; you do not do them properly. (*taking his hand*) That would have been a help to me.

(WACHSMUTH *nods and exits.* DR. STEINER *turns to* SAM.)

DR. STEINER   Sam, you wanted to ask me something.

SAM   I was deeply moved by what you said about Michaél and the dragon, and Michaél's mission. But then you had to answer so many questions from the members.

DR. STEINER   And you also had a question.

SAM   No, Herr Doctor. I always try not to burden you with my personal questions.

DR. STEINER   (*giving her his full attention*) Please, Sam, ask me your question.

SAM   (*hesitantly*) Well, during your lecture, I began to wonder: Who are you? Who were you? Who will you be?

DR. STEINER   (*drawing a curved-line figure*) If you ponder on who I am, with love and enthusiasm, you will find, even in this life, who I am.

SAM   Yes.—Oh, why do people treat you with such sweetness and sentimentality?

DR. STEINER   (*starting to laugh*) Sweetness? But there's nothing in me that would provoke sweetness or sentimentality.

SAM   Not *in* you, but everything gets projected as the opposite of what you want. You want freedom of thought, and what happens is the opposite. People make you into an authority that dominates them.

DR. STEINER   But I want people to be *free* and to think for themsel*ves*. And that depends on *them*.

SAM

But they don't *want* to think for themselves. You can't expect people to have what simply isn't in them.

DR. STEINER

That will pass. In two thousand years everything will be different. Remember what I said last time about *herring eggs*: ninety-nine out of a hundred die. If even half a person receives something from what is revealed, then it serves its purpose. Nature is wasteful. In the whole cosmos, the law of wastefulness prevails—yes, *wastefulness*.

(*They exit, as* WACHSMUTH *enters and sits.*)

(ITA WEGMAN'S *office at her medical clinic.* WACHSMUTH *is waiting for her.*)

ITA

(*storming in, then turning back for the last word in a heated discussion*) Whatever you lawyers say, having the laboratory next door to this clinic is indispensable. Our patients depend on it. *Pharmacies* depend on it. I can't see any other way than for our clinic to be absorbed into the laboratory corporation. (*turning to him*) Herr Wachsmuth. . .

WACHSMUTH

Dr. Steiner wanted me to speak to you. He has changed. It's not as easy as it once was to approach him. He seems heavily burdened.

ITA

Yes, I know. He used to laugh and light up like a child, even in serious moments. Now he is filled with life only when he lectures.

WACHSMUTH   I asked him how we can protect him—and the Society.

ITA   Well, for one thing, we can raise the money to rebuild the Goetheanum.

WACHSMUTH   That's not what I meant.

ITA   I understand you've also organized a watch.

WACHSMUTH   Well, yes. That as well. . .

ITA   Do we know who started the fire?

WACHSMUTH   No. There are suspicions, but . . .

ITA   So, the remaining buildings could still be in danger.

WACHSMUTH   Thirty young men have volunteered to guard them and to protect Herr Doctor's physical safety. But that's not why I'm here.

ITA   Oh. Is there something else you have in mind?

WACHSMUTH   I am seeking people who want to work together inwardly, with meditations Doctor Steiner would give to us.

ITA   He used to hold such lessons with us in Berlin. It was a private spiritual school. But he closed it when the war broke out, and he has not re-opened it.

WACHSMUTH   Perhaps it's time. If we could bring together a group of people who want to protect him, I think he will show us how to do it. Not for ourselves, but for the world.

ITA	If what you do is right, he will help you. If it's not, he won't, and you will have learned something.
WACHSMUTH	I am learning that it is difficult to reason with . . . someone close to him. But he wanted me to speak to you.
ITA	(*after an awkward moment*) We must keep our hearts warm. That's the only remedy that keeps us from becoming estranged from one another, even when opinions differ.
WACHSMUTH	You have a strong connection with him.
ITA	And *you* are now his personal assistant.
WACHSMUTH	He meets you here each morning.
ITA	He advises me with my patients.
WACHSMUTH	He also meets with you at evenings on the Hill.
ITA	He has long supported my initiatives. Now I want to actively serve his.
WACHSMUTH	Then will you join us?
ITA	I will wait until others are ready to see this need and can fully embrace it. To carry this through as if it were *my* will is out of the question.
WACHSMUTH	Very well. I will keep you informed.

(*Demon music. They exit.*)

❈

Scene 6: Resolve

The Grand Master *addresses his pupils. A* Green Demon *lurks and slithers among them. The* Secret Brother *looks on.*

Grand Master   Dear Brothers, the history of our brotherhood demands that we defend it, or we could lose our power in the world. At the beginning of the earth, exalted beings were sent down from higher realms to be the wise and watchful leaders of mankind. They cultivated in the sacred temples, out of the ranks of men, disciples, who, through renunciation and harsh tests, then proved mature enough to be initiated into the secret wisdom of these Mysteries. Those mighty teachers then withdrew, and their disciples, in their turn, selected men who could succeed them. And so it carried on from age to age. And to this day all genuine mystery schools descend directly from that earliest one. And we now cultivate within these walls that ancient lineage and must protect it.

(Music. Circular movement. The anticipated gathering in Haus Hansi. Miss Maryon *enters, then coughs terribly;* Ita *accompanies her off.* Marie *enters in her wheelchair;* Sam *helps her.* Dr. Steiner *enters.)*

Wachsmuth   Dr. Steiner, it's good to have you back in Dornach. It's very quiet here when you're away.

EHRENFRIED   People need the life your lectures waken in us.

WACHSMUTH   Herr Steffen published the essays you sent him for the newsletter. He was impressed you found the time to write them.

DR. STEINER   Herr Steffen works tirelessly for the Anthroposophical Society. And his poetic artistry is among its most beautiful treasures.

(*He greets* MARIE, *then crosses to greet* ITA.)

WACHSMUTH   (*aside to* EHRENFRIED) Ita Wegman has decided to join us after all. She has a strong connection with Dr. Steiner. But I wonder whether she really knows what she is doing.

ITA   (*speaking with* DR. STEINER) Dr. Steiner, a question is growing in my heart—about medical practice and research into hidden realities. I can't quite put it into words.

DR. STEINER   My dear Frau Doctor Wegman, when your question has ripened and you are able to formulate it, an answer will come.

(DR. STEINER *turns and addresses everyone in the room. He greets* ELISABETH VREEDE *warmly, but no one else seems to notice her.*)

DR. STEINER   Dear friends: You've gathered here in our home, of your own initiative, and at the invitation of Herr Doctor Wachsmuth—not because you are the most advanced pupils on the path of inner development. You are merely those who have found each other and have come together with a question, and that is what matters. (*they sit*) Some years ago, I gave up guiding such spiritual circles, because there was too little clear and wakeful consciousness—which such work *requires*. But once again it is now possible to make a start. We must develop the truly human forces of the "I Am." Throughout the ages, and even at the building of Solomon's Temple, the sons of Cain were builders and masons, while the sons of Abel were priests and monks. But the age-old strife and enmity between Cain and Abel continues. And these two opposing streams united only once: . . . in hatred of *the middle way* of the "I Am."

(*Music.* Michaél *appears wearing a tunic embroidered with a cross with seven red roses around it.*)

This union brought about the conflagration of the Goetheanum.

ELISABETH VREEDE

Oh!

EHRENFRIED   How terrible!

DR. STEINER   Yes, my friends: the fire occurred because the currents from both directions . . . united *against the middle.*

WACHSMUTH   What can we do?

(Michaél *moves.*)

DR. STEINER   Recognize what comes from the two directions. Be awake in confronting them. Wake up through right meditation! Meditating is not only a personal matter: it has meaning and importance for the world. The whole cosmos has an interest in whether we do it or we don't.

(*Music. Two* Green Demons *slither through.*)

You are sleeping in your thinking—and do not know it—and also in your feeling and your will! You are sleeping in your very self, your I!

(Michaél *banishes the demons.*)

Therefore, the spirit world has entrusted me with giving you this meditation:

(Michaél *gestures.*)

"O Man, know yourself!"
So sounds the Cosmic Word.

(*Gong. Music. Movement. Pupils exit.* Michaél *circles slowly.* Ita *and* Dr. Steiner *become* Reginald *and* Thomas Aquinas. Thomas *lies motionless on the bed, in his monastic cell.* Reginald *kneels beside him,* Michaél *still present.*)

Reginald (Ita) Thomas?—Thomas. (*no reply*) Brother Thomas, what happened? Did you see God?

Thomas (Dr. Steiner)
Perhaps.

(Michaél *withdraws.*)

Reginald You have been lying here in this ecstasy for three days now. Can we continue our work?

Thomas

No.

Reginald

What do you mean, no? Speak and I will write.

Thomas

Brother Reginald, I can't.

Reginald

You must. I've heard it said that when you were studying in Cologne, you were so quiet, your fellow students thought that you were slow, but then Albertus, your great teacher, said,

Albertus (Marie)

(*stepping onto a platform*) You call him the dumb ox, but one day he will produce such a bellowing that it will be heard throughout the world.

Reginald

You must finish your Great Work.

Thomas

I cannot.

Reginald

But why?

Thomas

Compared to what has been revealed to me, all that I have written seems like so much straw.

Reginald

Oh, Thomas, you *have* seen God.

Thomas

I have seen.

Reginald

And you have made up your mind.

Thomas

Dear Reginald, when I became a monk, my family hired a prostitute to tempt me. I drove her away with a smoldering log and swore a vow of everlasting chastity. Then I drew a cross on the wall with the ashes. I had made up my mind.

(*Music. Circular movement.* Albertus *exits.* Reginald *becomes* Ita, Thomas *becomes* Dr. Steiner. *Gong.* Ita *and the others sit in meditation.* Dr. Steiner *stands, aware of her awakening.*)

ITA   (*to herself, experiencing a vision like a dream*) What do I see?. . . Two monks in a monastic cell. A vow of chastity. . . And before this, I saw a young king in ancient times, grieving: He wrongfully killed a man—killed him in a drunken rage!—his faithful general and friend. And earlier, this same young king with his wise teacher, on a sacred island—Samothrace in the Aegean Sea.

(Michaél *appears.*)

Together they remembered former times, the burning of a temple. . . A deep impression lingers in my soul—of the Goddess of that temple. . . in Ephesus.

(Michaél *disappears. The* Grand Master, *holding a small bottle, and the* Secret Brother *appear on opposite sides.*)

SECRET BROTHER What is it you are asking me to do?

GRAND MASTER   This is a substance that was long since developed for this purpose. It will be your task to administer it to him.

SECRET BROTHER Oh! So, I am charged with poisoning Herr Steiner.

Grand Master   Because you're eas'ly inconspicuous, we've chosen you for this important task.

Secret Brother   But then, would this not set him free to work, perhaps more strongly, from the other side?

Grand Master   This poisoning is not intended to be fatal. (*handing him the bottle*) We do not want to *kill* him, but to put him into a state in which he will no longer control his clairvoyant capacities. They would be practically extinguished. We then can point to him and say, "You see? When you strive for spirit knowledge such as his, you will end up like this."

Secret Brother   Ah. And may I know how this substance works?

Grand Master   It is a secret herb. It strikes digestion, disrupts life forces, and it blocks clairvoyance, causing a serious *mental crisis*.

(*Meditants open their eyes, heads turn.* Secret Brothers *exit.*)

❧

SCENE 7: ONWARD

DR. STEINER

What we have accomplished so far should be only a beginning. Each person's work should flow into the others' and be joyfully acknowledged.

(*The meditants begin to exit.*)

But when I work and nothing happens, I am lamed. (*now alone with* MARIE, *sitting down beside her*) For years it's caused me greatest pain that many of our members are like sacks of flour, as if they have lead weights around their feet.

MARIE

I, for one, manage to do my work in spite of my feet.

DR. STEINER

Yes, my dear Mouse, you, Herr Steffen, Dr. Wegman, Miss Maryon—and other truly active and productive individuals—should be recognized and given the support you need. (*standing*) But the Society, as a whole, sleeps on. There seems to be no way to waken it to action.

MARIE

Well, I hope you can waken the Stuttgart members.

DR. STEINER

I'm only going to Stuttgart to meet with the teachers at the Waldorf School.

MARIE

Dear Heart, don't give up on the Society. It depends on you! (*with increasing fire*) And another thing: for women, there is even more at stake. Something miraculous has happened: Women have been given the one thing that has been withheld from them. In this time of moral decay, of dulled thinking, of the crassest egotism, *teachings* that had been hidden in the mystery temples and given only to a few have come into the open for the whole human race—*through you*; (*he stands*) teachings that could open new organs of perception and raise humanity from spiritual desolation to actual spirit experience. A path of knowledge (*he takes a notebook out of his pocket*), a way of knowing what is thought to be unknowable and applying that knowledge to actual life. Women are now allowed to participate in this work. For the first time, since spirit knowledge has been given to humankind, they may receive this knowledge in common with men, and work together to inaugurate a new era. (*he takes her hand for a moment, then leaves the room; she follows him.*) If you separate yourself from the Society, that opportunity will be lost!

(SAM *enters.*)

(*continuing loudly offstage*) You can do better than that. You have been working at this for so long.

(SAM *looks toward the "door," embarrassed.*)

MARIE   (*offstage*) Oh, you are such a stubborn mule!

(DR. STEINER *re-enters, with his notebook.*)

DR. STEINER   (*seeing* SAM; *somewhat sheepishly, he looks back at*

the door, then at Sam *and, with a loving shrug. . .)*
That's just the way she is.

Sam   I thought she was giving an elocution lesson to one of her students.

Dr. Steiner   *(smiling)* No, it's just me.

Sam   Herr Doctor, I was so embarrassed last night. I really don't know how my cat got into your lecture. I am so sorry.

Dr. Steiner   Oh, it's no problem. She has already become a member. Look. Here is her membership card.

             (He takes a ball of yarn out of his pocket and tosses it to Sam, *who misses it. It rolls away on the floor and off the stage.)*

             Oh! Let's see who can get it first.

             (They both scurry on the floor after the ball, playing and laughing. Marie *enters in her wheelchair.)*

Marie   And those *Brownshirt thugs* in Germany are only proving how important your work is, when they disrupt your lectures and *(seeing them, nonplussed)* threaten your life! What are you doing down there on the floor with Sam?

Dr. Steiner   *(still on the floor)* I have to be able to play sometimes, and I can only do it with people I know will play along with me.

Marie   Well, don't miss your train. Sam, here is my watch. I'll need it repaired before we leave for England.

SAM　　England. And. . .

(WACHSMUTH *enters with two umbrellas, which he and* SAM *open.* [DR. STEINER *exits.*])

Wales!

(*Penmaenmawr, Wales. Outdoors.* MARIE *in her wheelchair, with* SAM *and* WACHSMUTH.)

MARIE　　The modern world just vanishes in these surroundings—in this little Welsh mining village. Penmaenmawr, in Dwygyfylchi, near Llanfairfechan. I will not rest until I find my way into the sound of the Celtic tongue. Just listen to the way the words reflect the landscape: (*having them repeat after her*) Llanfairfechan, Dwygyfylchi. Oh, where is Dr. Steiner? I'd like to share all this with him.

SAM　　Has he sneaked off up the mountain again, to the standing stones?

WACHSMUTH　　Probably. I climbed up there with him yesterday, but Dr. Wegman hadn't arrived yet.

MARIE　　Ah. Yes, of course. She seems to have made a connection with him. He'll want to show the Druid-circle to *her*.

SAM　　Frau Doctor, are you jealous?

MARIE　　Me? Jealous? No. Of course not. But I *am* sorry I can't walk up the mountain myself.

SAM　　Oh, Frau Doctor, you used to be so agile and light on your feet. What happened?

MARIE

Sam, please don't ask about the pain in my legs. There is no *physical* explanation.

(*Celtic music. Circular movement.* SAM, MARIE, *and* WACHSMUTH *exit.* DR. STEINER *and* ITA *enter.*)

(*Mountain plateau. The mighty remains of a druid stone circle.*)

DR. STEINER

Look over the edges of the stones. You see the peaks of the mountains in the distance? In their Hibernian Mysteries, the Druids gazed over these stones, at those mountains—and at the constellations moving through the seasons.

ITA

Was stargazing the purpose of these standing stones?

DR. STEINER

Yes. Just think: instead of printing-presses, they had these stone circles so they could read the secrets of the cosmos and guide the people in religion and culture, in the management of crops and farming and with healing medicines. Listen. Wonders of primeval wisdom are still radiating here. Cosmic memories hover like luminous clouds in the hollows of these hilltops. And even now, the effects of nature are rising up from the earth, living in the air and beaming down from the sun.

ITA

And just an hour ago these beams of light broke through a storm of pouring rain!

DR. STEINER

Look! There's a cheeky elemental making faces right behind you.

(*He puts his thumb on his nose and wiggles his fingers at the elemental, then dodges as it runs past his feet.*)

ITA   You're joking!

DR. STEINER   No, I'm not. They're all around us here, and they awaken memories of nature beings that the *Druids* could see—giants of frost and storm and fire. (*stepping onto a spot in the middle of the stage*) Just think, thousands of years ago the Druid sages stood here in this very place, the priest before his altar in the dark of the stones. His breathing changed, his pulse changed, and the greatest secrets were revealed to him in tidal waves of knowledge—especially in midsummer.

ITA   You speak as though you are seeing all this right now—at this very moment.

DR. STEINER   Yes, I am. Other Mysteries I could research at a distance, but I couldn't see all this until I came here.

ITA   (*cautiously, with reverence*) Dr. Steiner: Could medicine once again be as it was in ancient times, filled with living spirit wisdom and deep humanity? Couldn't we bring the Mysteries to life again in a way that's fitting for our time?

(*He smiles knowingly and gestures, inviting her to stand on the spot where he was standing. She does.*)

Oh! Oh (*quietly, having a sudden vision*), how could I have been so blind? Even in ancient times you were my teacher. In many lives, in many places I have asked such questions. As Gilgamesh asked Eabani in Chaldea, I asked by the River Tigris.

DR. STEINER　　(*he smiles and nods*) Yes.

Ita　　As the temple maiden Mysa asked wise Cratylus, I asked in Ephesus.

DR. STEINER　　(*he smiles and nods*) Yes.

Ita　　As Alexander asked his teacher Aristotle, I asked on the isle of Samothrace. (*He nods*)

As Brother Reginald asked Thomas Aquinas, I asked in the monastic cell.

(MICHAËL *appears, wearing the rose cross.*)

DR. STEINER　　(*friendly nod*) And on the Dornach hill, your soul must find itself with courage, so you perceive how spirit sun shadowlessly weaves the true red glow of dawn around the stars of the Rosy Cross.

ITA　　Karma—completely revealed to my soul. I understand.

DR. STEINER　　The spirit world rejoices. The Mysteries shall come to life again.

(*Music.* MICHAËL *rejoices with a ritual gesture.*)

End of Act I

Act II

SCENE 1: VOLCANO

DR. STEINER   (*addressing the audience*) We can only respond
with our spiritual worldview to the suffering we
see in today's civilization—if we know what's ac-
tually happening in the world. So, wake up and
become conscious that you are sleeping! With
each awakening, we come into a new sphere of
the world, for we live completely surrounded
by such spheres in vast abundance. But, merely
sleeping, we know nothing of them.

(SAM *enters. Morning. November 10, 1923. Outside the Goetheanum ruins.*)

SAM   Something happened while I was here on watch
duty the other night. I was walking around the
ruins, and suddenly, I stood here on this path,
spellbound. I had a vision of Berlin... in flames!
I saw your home there, the entire city, in ruins.

DR. STEINER   Yes, Sam. Such things will come...

SAM   Oh, Herr Doctor, could you give our friends in
Berlin some helpful words for when hard times
come and we no longer have you with us.

(WACHSMUTH *enters in a hurry.*)

WACHSMUTH   Dr. Steiner, have you seen today's news? (*handing him a newspaper*) The National Socialists attempted a coup in Germany yesterday.

SAM   Oh! In Berlin?

WACHSMUTH   No, in Munich. (*he exits*)

(DR. STEINER *reads.*)

SAM   Berlin could be next.

DR. STEINER   Sam, please come for tea this afternoon! I will give you something.

(*Gong. He exits.* MARIE *enters in her wheelchair. Haus Hansi.*)

MARIE   He seemed to take your request very seriously.

SAM   Frau Doctor, I know he won't be with us much longer.

MARIE   Oh no, I am fully confident that he will be with us for long years to come.

SAM   No. We will lose him. He will die. And we will no longer have him here.

(DR. STEINER *enters with several papers under his arm. A moment; he has heard her.*)

DR. STEINER   Sam, I have to ask you to travel to Berlin this evening to see to some urgent business.

SAM   (*surprised*) But Herr Doctor, I was hoping to stay here in Dornach for the next few days. . .

DR. STEINER   This is the lease on the Berlin apartments. I have written to the branch secretary asking her to give notice to give them up. We must vacate the building there immediately—our residence, the offices, and the Hall.

Sam	(*shocked*) No!
Dr. Steiner	Yes. Sam, you must do this for my sake.
Marie	But we *built* that Hall! Must we really give it up?
Dr. Steiner	Yes, Frau Steiner, and move all our books and inventory. If these men come to power, Berlin will fall, great devastation will descend on Central Europe, and neither of us will be able to set foot on German soil again.
Sam	If only your ideas for social life had been taken seriously after the war.
Dr. Steiner	We are on top of a volcano that could erupt at any moment, if there are not enough spiritual powers on earth to prevent it.
Sam	(*solemnly*) I will take the night train to Berlin. And I will fulfill your commission.
Dr. Steiner	(*handing* Sam *a verse*) I have also written this verse for you for our friends in Berlin. Sam, there is much suffering in these words, and the hour will come when our Berlin friends will read between the lines—of even worse sufferings. Tell them I will then be there among them. Sam, remain courageous and faithful.
	(Sam *exits.* Marie *and* Dr. Steiner *look at each other. Then* Marie *wheels upstage—and remains, her back turned—as* Ita *enters.*)

❋

Scene 2: Unbroken Thread

The studio.

DR. STEINER — The members don't understand how to work together. They lack will. The Society is half dead. It's riddled with demonic holes! Perhaps I will have to start all over again with spiritual work in a small group. We could then work outwardly in the world, without the burden of a Society.

ITA — But you spoke last summer of establishing a school *within* the Society, under your leadership. A Michaél school for *new* Mysteries, welcoming students from all walks of life.

DR. STEINER — Yes, Dr. Wegman, if you are willing to help me, then I will dare to do it! But it is a great risk, breaking ancient spiritual tradition by combining my inner work with outer administration.

ITA — Don't you have to remain independent of the Society's administration? As a teacher, you've always been our guest.

DR. STEINER — That would change. I would have to take the Society into my own hands and rebuild it.

ITA — The members look up to you as a great Master.

DR. STEINER — I would also become united with them as a fellow member.

ITA	Would the spirit world support this and stand by you?
DR. STEINER	I don't know. But the consequences would fall entirely on me.
ITA	Do you mean that you could lose your spiritual capacities?
DR. STEINER	Yes. In earlier times, before the deed of Christ, anyone who took such an action would have to pay for it with sudden death. But now the state of humankind demands the courage and the trust to do such tremendous things: to call upon the elements and the angelic hierarchies, to found new Mysteries, not handed down from the gods, but through *human relationships*. A great deal depends on how the members will respond. It will either mean everything to them, or nothing.
ITA	And if they fail to develop spiritually and it doesn't mean everything to them?
DR. STEINER	Then karma will hold sway, and a terrible regression would occur.
ITA	I will stand by you, whatever happens and whatever you decide.
DR. STEINER	Yes, you and I have found the turning point of our destiny: in primordial times, at the edge of the abyss, and on spirit heights. It forges the resolve never to lose each other.

(*Gong.*)

Dr. Steiner   Looking back along the course of time, I find the sweetly mild Mysa, in the light of Ephesus' Mystery Temple, her gentle being tenderly pondering, weaving among the images of gods.

(Music. Circular movement. Finger chimes. Dr. Steiner becomes Cratylus. Ita becomes Mysa. As if walking side by side as they talk:)

Mysa (Ita)

We now approach the Goddess' hallowed Temple gates.
Soon night will bear our souls away on separate paths,
as moonlight glimmers on the Bay of Ephesus.

Cratylus (Dr. Steiner)

And you reflect to me our goddess Artemis,
for you are thriving in her sacred mystery school.

Mysa

When we awake from sleep, may we converse again?

Cratylus

We will then speak of what we have experienced—
you from the depths of the Goddess,
I from the heights of the Word.

Mysa

Oh Cratylus, my teacher, how am I to grasp
the things that you behold in the vast cosmos?

Cratylus

Know that my heart shines warmly on your being, Mysa.
The gods of Hades may destroy this sacred temple,
but our eternal destiny cannot be shaken.

(*Symbolic gestures. Music. Circular movement.
Gong.* Cratylus *becomes* Dr. Steiner. Mysa
becomes Ita *and remains visible, her back turned.*
Marie *turns in her wheelchair and speaks.*)

(*Haus Hansi.*)

Marie	Why not appoint Herr Steffen, our great Swiss Poet!? He too approaches life with artistic sensitivity. And he is *young.*
Dr. Steiner	I need *you* as my vice-chairman. The spirit world endowed you with cosmic forces and has decreed that I can only fulfill my earthly task *with you.*
Marie	But I want to dedicate the remaining years of my life to *our new arts* of *speech* and *eurythmy.* You have told me many times that that is the task for which I was destined.
Dr. Steiner	You should also assume with me the *leadership* of the *new* Society.
Marie	I am just not up to taking on responsibility for both the Society and the artistic work.
Dr. Steiner	Your artistic work must continue in our new Michaél School for Spiritual Science.
Marie	I will lead a performing arts Section in the new School. But I don't know how much longer I still have in this life. I often pray that I will die before you do.
Dr. Steiner	No, my dear, you will have to outlive me by twenty years.

MARIE

That is a terrible thought! You are always healthy and strong; *I* am the sickly one!

(SAM *brings* DR. STEINER *a cane and exits.*)

DR. STEINER

Yes, my dear, (*handing her the cane*) you must live twenty years longer in order to preserve my work. That is your karma.

MARIE

My karma! (*she takes the cane and stands up, with effort*) In any case, in the eyes of the outer world, it would be unseemly for an international society such as ours to have a husband-and-wife team, "Mr. and Mrs. Steiner," as its chairman and vice-chairman.

DR. STEINER

Well, then I will name Herr Steffen as vice-chairman. But the will of the spirit world must be respected. Herr Steffen can only assume this position jointly with you.

MARIE

All right. Who else will serve on the executive council with us?

DR. STEINER

Miss Maryon will lead a Sculptural Arts Section, but understandably, she has declined to be on the Council. Her health is in very critical condition. So I'd like to ask Fräulein Doctor Vreede to join the Council—and also to lead a Section for Mathematics and Astronomy.

MARIE

Fräulein Doctor Vreede?! She's Dutch, isn't she? What qualifications does *she* have?

DR. STEINER

She is a doctor of philosophy. And she has dedicated her life completely to our cause. People don't notice her because she was born outside her karmic group, but she has been tried and tested to the utmost.

MARIE

Very well, but a new beginning needs young people.

DR. STEINER

Yes. I plan to ask Dr. Wachsmuth to be the cashier.

MARIE

I think he would prefer to be called "treasurer."

DR. STEINER

(*with humor*) A fancy title does not make it more important. — And Frau Doctor Wegman will serve as secretary.

MARIE

Ita Wegman?

DR. STEINER

Yes. She will also lead a Medical Section. Will that be difficult for you?

MARIE

For me? No, of course not. What do I know about medicine? But it will certainly stir up some resistance from the other *doctors*.

DR. STEINER

If the agitation and propaganda against Frau Doctor Wegman continues, it will lead to the shattering of the new Society.

(ITA *turns. Circular movement.* SAM *pushes the empty wheelchair and* MARIE *exits with the cane.*)

(*The studio. Evening.* DR. STEINER *and* ITA *are in the midst of a profound conversation.*)

DR. STEINER

My dear Mysa-Ita, our karma is a thread of friendship, through many lives and through millennia. It can also become a foundation for our new Society. Hundreds of people will be coming here from all over the world for our founding meeting during Christmas. May I speak to them of Gilgamesh and Eabani, of Cratylus and Mysa?

ITA   Yes, of course. You've spoken of such history before. And will you also speak of Aristotle and his pupil, and of Thomas and his friend Reginald?

DR. STEINER   I must now trace a long unbroken thread of ancient lineage, not through the sacred mystery temples, but through successive lives—of *these two souls.*

ITA   But you won't tell them that you are speaking of *yourself*—and of me, will you?

DR. STEINER   No, I mustn't. People must be free to discover that themselves.

ITA   Should they—discover it?

DR. STEINER   It would be good if more people could wake up to these connections—and also grasp their own karmic threads.

ITA   But will they?

DR. STEINER   Hearts will grasp karma when they learn to read the word that fashions human life, when they learn to speak the word that fashions the human being.

(Sacred moment. Music. DR. STEINER *exits. Circular movement.)*

Scene 3: Open Secrets

The carpentry shop. Ita, Wachsmuth, Ehrenfried, Sam, Elisabeth Wreede, *and, finally, the* Secret Brother. Marie *enters with a cane and sits.* Dr. Steiner *shakes hands with* Wachsmuth, *sees the* Secret Brother, *then steps onto the platform.* (Miss Maryon *is not present.*)

Dr. Steiner Just as the fire of Ephesus flared up anew within the hearts of Aristotle and young Alexander (*tears quietly stream from* Ita's *eyes*), a spiritual flame shall light up in our hearts to shed new light and warmth on all that we resolve to carry forward on the advancing wave of world evolving.—My dear friends, you welcomed me today by rising in memory of the Goetheanum, which was taken from us one year ago this very night. Let us now rise in token that we vow to keep on working in the *spirit* of the Goetheanum, with all the best and highest forces that we have within us.

(*All stand or step forward.*)

So it shall be.

And we will hold to this our solemn vow. We will be true to it as long as we are able and with all our will.

My dear friends, you have now laid in your hearts the foundation stone for the universally human, all-encompassing Anthroposophical Society. And so, I ask you to carry your warm hearts into the world to do powerful healing work. And help will be given to you, enlightening your heads for what you would guide with focused will. This is what we must undertake with all our strength.

(*Informal conversations.* Sam *serves tea and cakes. Music. Lights shift. The* Secret Brother *removes the bottle of poison from his pocket and pours it into a cup of tea, as the others stand upstage, backs turned.*)

GRAND MASTER (*stepping onto a platform*) It is an herb. It strikes digestion and it blocks clairvoyance, causing a serious mental crisis.

(*Eerie music continues, as* Dr. Steiner *crosses to the* Secret Brother *and accepts the tea. The* Secret Brother *goes out, unnoticed.* Dr. Steiner *drinks the tea. The music stops.* Dr. Steiner *moans and staggers.* Sam *rushes to him. Lights shift gradually.*)

DR. STEINER Oh, I feel awful.

SAM Oh, Herr Doctor! Here. Sit down. I'll find Frau Doctor and Dr. Wegman.

DR. STEINER (*holding her hand tightly*) Oh, no, stay with me. Water, please. Water. Ohhh.

(Ehrenfried *rushes to them.*)

EHRENFRIED What has happened?

DR. STEINER (*in terrible pain*) I have been poisoned.

SAM

(*to* EHRENFRIED) Go get help. He's cold as ice and bathed in sweat.

(EHRENFRIED *exits with teacups.*)

MARIE

(*turning*) Has something happened? (*Seeing* DR. STEINER *and going to him*) What's wrong? What has happened?

DR. STEINER

I have been poisoned—how are the other Council members?

MARIE

They're fine. But I felt uneasy that you were absent for so long.

DR. STEINER

Have any of you drunk anything?

MARIE

No.

ITA

(*turning*) No. I'm fine.

(EHRENFRIED *returns with a glass of water.*)

DR. STEINER

And Fräulein Vreede?

ELISABETH VREEDE

(*turning*) I'm fine. And Herr Steffen, too.

SAM *gives* DR. STEINER *the glass of water and steps back.*

DR. STEINER

Has anything happened to Wachsmuth?

(WACHSMUTH *turns.*)

ITA

No. He's right here. He's perfectly all right.

(WACHSMUTH *goes to him.*)

DR. STEINER   Good. It's only me, then.

WACHSMUTH   (*starting to go*) I'll go call a doctor.

DR. STEINER   No. No. Absolutely not. Don't tell anyone.

ITA   What can we do for you?

DR. STEINER   Just bring me some milk.

(ELISABETH VREEDE *nods and goes out.*)

And promise me you won't call a doctor. Dr. Wegman is here. Don't tell anyone else. Absolutely no one.

(ITA *sits with him.*)

WACHSMUTH   All right. I promise. No one will find out about this. No doctor. No one.

DR. STEINER   Bring me all the milk we have.

(SAM *rushes out.*)

MARIE   As if struck down by a sword!

(EHRENFRIED *takes the empty glass from* DR. STEINER *and goes out.*)

GRAND MASTER   (*still on the platform, observing*) How did you do it?

SECRET BROTHER   (*beneath him*) I slipped it easily into his tea. No one noticed, I'm sure.

GRAND MASTER   And are you sure he drank it?

SECRET BROTHER   Absolutely certain. He turned pale and left the room.

(*They exit. Music. Movement. All exit.* Ita *enters with* Miss Maryon *and helps her into her sick-bed.*)

(*Midnight.* Ita Wegman's *clinic.*)

MISS MARYON   When will Herr Doctor come?

ITA   I don't know. (*sitting in the chair beside her*) Do you feel you can breathe now?

MISS MARYON   Yes. It's better. I need to speak with him.

ITA   He's been delayed

MISS MARYON   Is he ill?

ITA   His digestion is bad.

MISS MARYON   People are saying—that he was poisoned.

ITA   He is recovering.

MISS MARYON   You've been so attentive—caring for him—and for me.

ITA   It could not be otherwise, Miss Maryon.

MISS MARYON   Once—on the scaffold, as we were sculpting—he nearly fell—onto a sharp post below.

ITA   Oh! What happened?

MISS MARYON   I caught hold of him.

ITA   You saved his life.

MISS MARYON   You—must also—

ITA   Yes, I know.

MISS MARYON   How can he keep on working?

ITA   He draws on spirit forces in order to go on.

MISS MARYON   I can't. I'm so weak, I'm no longer able to wait until he comes.

(*She becomes calm. Without fight, without pain, death comes softly and sublimely. Sustained note on the cello.* DR. STEINER *enters with a suitcase.* MISS MARYON *gets out of bed, faces him for a moment, and goes out.*)

(*The* GRAND MASTER *and* SECRET BROTHER *appear at their platform.*)

GRAND MASTER   The poison isn't having the effect that we intended.

SECRET BROTHER   Perhaps it takes some time.

GRAND MASTER   (*vehemently*) It's been months. His work's continuing unhindered. In fact, it has increased. He's given almost ninety lectures in the past twelve weeks. He's opened up a spiritual school with sections for the sciences and arts. He's teaching courses now, describing former lives of noted figures. Thousands of people flock to him.

SECRET BROTHER   It doesn't sound like he's in *mental crisis,* does it?

GRAND MASTER   He's dangerous! More now than ever. Because of him we're losing strength. He's draining power from our rituals. Sacred initiation rites depend on secrecy, which he has breached.

(They exit. Dr. Steiner picks up his suitcase, Ita still sitting. They remain at a distance from each other throughout the scene.)

Scene 4: Breakthrough

The studio.

ITA

I'm worried that this course for the farmers may be too much for you. It's a full schedule and a long journey—into Germany, where there have been threats on your life.

DR. STEINER

I hope nothing bad will happen. And I will try to maintain my health. But this has to go forward; it might soon no longer be possible.

ITA

Please be careful. I wish I could go with you, but there's so much to be attended to at the clinic.

DR. STEINER

You will be near to me in soul, as a friend in spirit worlds. It is in our karma that I must find in you a real, unwavering friend, if your path of development is to go entirely in the right way.

ITA

Why did it take so long to truly find each other in this life? Only now I recognize what ancient karma was renewed between us in Munich, all those years ago.

DR. STEINER

(*having put down his suitcase*) It was not yet time. You had to let it settle in you first, forget it all again, while you completed your medical studies.

ITA

But I could have come to Dornach ten years ago.

DR. STEINER

It would not have been right for you to abandon your work in Zürich any sooner. It was, after all, a bridge between spiritual science and conventional medicine. And you had other karma to resolve in Zürich.

ITA

It seems so tragic.

DR. STEINER

If this karma must have a tragic streak for now, in the future it will not be possible for there to be any hindrances at all. Our friendship rests on the most unshakable rock: It rests, after all, on what your being reveals to me. And that is much, very much.

ITA

Whatever is unconnected to you pales in comparison.

DR. STEINER

But my dear Mysa, I could not relate to anyone as I do to you. You get to know me in ways that are so different from how others know me.

ITA

And soon you'll have to go. (*sitting down on the bed*) The car will be here to take you to the train.

DR. STEINER

You parted from *me* once long ago, for an all-embracing life of active deeds. We had unfurled far-reaching plans before our souls, and you, Alexander, set out to realize those plans in your own way.

ITA

To realize those plans, I also did much harm.

DR. STEINER   There was no other way for it to happen than by your doing harm to many people.

ITA   But I also hurt you.

DR. STEINER   A great deal was taken from me when you departed. Youth, which in you stood by my side, was taken from me. I had grown old. I was never so old in any other lifetime. (*standing*) My heart went with you across the Hellespont. That was my mood, as you departed to the Black Sea and beyond.

ITA   I tried to put your teachings into action. But I wrongly killed a man—in a drunken rage—my faithful general and friend.

DR. STEINER   He confronted you. To begin with, his behavior toward you was unjustified. But then you did him wrong. That was a karmic debt. Now it is resolved.

ITA   Did we have to wait until that karma was resolved?

DR. STEINER   What would have happened between us, if that weren't so? That is something I often asked myself about our tragedy, even before you spoke to me so beautifully.

ITA   I knew you were my teacher; I knew even before you spoke to me in Munich.

DR. STEINER   . . . seventeen years ago. That mood of age came over me again and just as strongly. Suddenly you were there, sitting in the conference hall. And I felt intensely weary. This weariness was the karmic image of my age when you departed from me. Now all that is no more.

Ita   Yes. That is all past.

Dr. Steiner   And because of you, I can now speak to people in a different way. I'm supported more and more by the love I foster for your highly cherished soul.

(*Car horn.*)

Herr Meyer is waiting. (*picking up his suitcase*) I wish we could continue talking.

Ita   It's not always good to say everything.

Dr. Steiner   Yes, it *is* good, when you speak to me as you have spoken.

(*Music. He exits.*)

(*She exits, as the* Grand Master *and the* Secret Brother *enter and sit on their platform,* Green Demons *hovering around them. Music.*)

Secret Brother   Exalted Master, you said that he is draining power from our rituals. Please forgive my asking, but is the power of your spirit vision also dimming?

Grand Master   (*reflecting*) I can still see—down in the cold dark place of truth, where we receive instruction for our work—that, though the fire should have killed him and the poison, silenced him, swarms of unseen forces will work on. His followers will turn against each other, (*standing*) and in the wake of world catastrophes, he'll be forgotten. (*he exits*)

(*Music.* Dr. Steiner *enters and reaches out across the stage to the* Secret Brother. *They nearly shake hands, but the* Secret Brother *cowers and leaves.*)

(*The studio.* Dr. Steiner *is wearing a rose-cross pendant. He writes on a slip of paper, as* Green Demons *slither near his ear. Then,* Ita *enters. Lights up.*)

ITA

Oh, thank goodness! You got home safely.

DR. STEINER

I left the farm on Tuesday, finished things off in Jena on Wednesday, accomplished what was necessary in Stuttgart, and here I am with you again in Dornach.

(*He hands her the slip of paper.*)

ITA

What's this?

DR. STEINER

It's a message that I wrote down, from the anti–Michaél demons.

ITA

(*reading*) "If you fail to carry out what's necessary by the stroke of Michaél, we will arrive at the Four."—The Four?

DR. STEINER

The number four is an expression for the physical world. It means that a breakthrough for Michaél's work must be achieved before Michaelmas, or else the demons will attack my physical body—and I will become ill.

ITA   What! Now *this* as well! What can I do?

DR. STEINER   We must follow through with our intentions.

                   (*Music.* DEMONS *come in. Lights shift.*)

                   The demons are hard at work, making jeering threats to rush in and attack if we do not succeed. They hurl themselves recklessly into their efforts to destroy Michaél's work.

ITA   What are these demons?

DR. STEINER   They are spirits of darkness. You have met them on your spirit path—green and jealous minions of the dragon. Klingsor and his fiendish hordes are also among them.

ITA   I have experienced many of these threats. I've partly understood and partly not. I know that much still remains hidden from me.

DR. STEINER   They conceal their intentions, but only we can wrest their secrets from them. Only human beings, and not the gods, can gain any knowledge of them. They hide in a place of darkness where even the light trembles, proclaiming these riddles. Our wrestling souls can find each other there and offer the demons' secrets to the waiting gods. Then light may grow where, without this deed, eternal darkness would prevail.

ITA   Such a place exists.

DR. STEINER   It must vanish.

(*Music.* Michaél *appears wearing the rose-cross tunic. Lights up. The* Demons *disperse.*)

Michaél's gaze admonishes our souls to one day make that place of darkness vanish.

Ita I must go forward. How can my soul find yours in that place of darkness?

Michaél (*to her, gesturing with offstage voice*)
If you will follow him with love,
then his companions in the spirit
will guide you on your spirit path.
We need his path-of-spirit's great expanse.
He needs your being's escort in the dance.

(Ita *steps forward.*)

Ita Yes! I am a pupil in the light of Michaél,

Dr. Steiner in time and in eternity.

(*She faces him.* Dr. Steiner *removes the rose-cross pendant from around his neck and places it around hers.*)

I now admit you to the spirit circle.

(Michaél *gestures.*)

From this moment onward we are both there for the Michaél School together—(*They stand side by side*)—in unified work of soul.

(Michaél *exits. Music. Movement.* Dr. Steiner *becomes ill.* Ita *helps him into bed.*)

❧

Scene 5: The Great Work

The carpentry shop. Ehrenfried, Ita, Wachsmuth, *and* Elisabeth Vreede.

Ehrenfried	(*pacing across the stage*) He hasn't come up the hill in two days, and tomorrow will be Michaelmas!
Wachsmuth	I'm sorry, Herr Pfeiffer, but Herr Steffen has announced that a*ll* of Dr. Steiner's obligations are canceled until further notice.
Ehrenfried	All right, I'll tell the farmers that he won't be able to meet with them.
Wachsmuth	What else can we say? He's exhausted. He was intensely busy in his travels all summer. And he has given over sixty lectures here in the last few weeks—often three or four a day! (*he steps upstage*)
Ita	He's pouring forth his whole life's work in an effort to awaken us, to lift us up out of our ordinary consciousness.
Wachsmuth	Anyone can see how ill he is. Before he lectures, he can barely stand.
Ehrenfried	But when he takes his place onstage, he is dynamic and full of life.
Ita	He says the lecturing keeps him healthy. What tires him is people's incomprehension.

Their dead thoughts leave him paralyzed.

EHRENFRIED   He's just overdone it. Lectures to the doctors and the priests, the teachers, scientists, artists, and actors, as well as for the workers and builders. Then evening history for the members.

WACHSMUTH   (*to* ITA) And he was visiting your patients in the clinic in between.

ITA   Yes, we carefully calculated how much strength he had for all that.

ELISABETH VREEDE
    (*quietly stepping forward*) But then four hundred people wanted to meet with him personally, and he refused to turn a single soul away.

WACHSMUTH   That was too much.

ITA   (*crossing the stage*) Yes, that *was* too much. I think we have to admit that we're not yet succeeding in protecting him with meditation and inner work.

ELISABETH VREEDE
    Or in carrying the spirit of the Goetheanum in our hearts.

WACHSMUTH   (*stepping upstage of her*) Dr. Wegman, are you suggesting that you have the capacity to judge such things?

ITA   Well, I do feel I have a responsibility for inner work—as his colleague in the Michaél School.

WACHSMUTH	He gave all of us on the *Council* responsibility for the School. But *you* seem to be spending more time with him than any of us.
ITA	We are writing a book together.
WACHSMUTH	Are you writing in German or in Dutch?
ITA	In German, of course.
WACHSMUTH	Well, I wouldn't have expected *you* to write a book.
ITA	Of course, *Herr Steffen* is the poet and author. I am a physician.
WACHSMUTH	And you are also Dr. *Steiner's* physician. Can you tell us what is ailing him?
ITA	Primarily his lower abdomen. It's extremely difficult for him to digest anything.
WACHSMUTH	Was he poisoned on New Year's Day?
ITA	Yes. He was. But that's not what's ailing him now.
WACHSMUTH	What does *he* say about the poisoning?
ITA	He doesn't speak about it.
WACHSMUTH	*Someone* is speaking about it.
ITA	What do you mean?
WACHSMUTH	Rumors are circulating again.
ITA	These rumors *themselves* are poisonous for him.

WACHSMUTH   There are also other rumors.

ITA   Other rumors?

WACHSMUTH   We wouldn't want to accuse you of spreading speculation about *your own* past lives. But some people are interpreting what Dr. Steiner said at Christmas, about successive lives of two connected souls, to…

(Urgent knocking. Pause. They all look at the door.)

Come in.

(SAM comes in through the doorway.)

SAM   Excuse me. I've just come up the hill from Frau Doctor. Dr. Steiner intends to leave his sickbed today after all.

(DR. STEINER carefully gets out of his bed.)

Herr Meyer will drive him up the hill, and he *will deliver his lecture*!

(SAM exits, WACHSMUTH and EHRENFRIED exit, ITA helps DR. STEINER out, and ELISABETH VREEDE is left alone. She speaks directly to the audience.)

ELISABETH VREEDE

(strongly, from her heart) A mighty stream of truly spiritual life is flowing through our movement now, and Dr. Steiner seems to be recovering, but it is a difficult and painful time for our Executive Council. Discord and antipathies rise up among us. — Our movement is based on *people. Human beings*

and *relationships* must create the character of our Society and School. A spiritual movement cannot come into the world in any other way; it must be permeated with the heart's blood.

(*Circular movement. Music builds.*)

(*The carpentry shop.* Elisabeth Vreede *sits down with* Wachsmuth, Ita, Ehrenfried, *and* Sam. Dr. Steiner *addresses them and the audience, inwardly battling demons, which surround him.*)

Dr. Steiner   And then, after you have gone through the gate of death, you will find in the spirit world all those with whom you shall prepare the Great Work, to lead humanity beyond the enormous crisis of this century.

(Demons *move. Music. Lights darken.*)

This work is: to let the power of Michaél's Being and Will penetrate the whole of human life.

(Demons *attack. Always upright, he falters slightly.*)

Ehrenfried   (*standing up momentarily with* Wachsmuth) He's fainting!

Dr. Steiner   Only if this power is able to overcome (*again he falters*) . . .truly overcome the demons and the dragon—and you know well what that is—if you receive this with true and faithful hearts and tender love, and make it live in your deeds in all its strength, then you will be worthy helpers of what now has to enter earthly evolution.

> (*He nearly collapses. The* Demons *move in. For a moment, it seems that he could faint.*)

Ehrenfried   (*standing up again with* Wachsmuth) Dr. Steiner!

> (*The* Demons *disperse. Lights brighten.*)

Dr. Steiner   My dear friends, I don't have sufficient strength to say much more this evening. May these few words speak to your soul in such a way that you receive this thought of Michaél as he appears clothed in the rays of the sun, and points us toward what must now take place. So, let this verse be my closing words to you today:

> (*Music.* Michaél *appears.*)

(*addressing spirit-powers, as* Michaél *gestures*)
You, shining Spirit-powers
who spring from forces of the Sun,
blessing all Worlds,
you are predestined
to be the radiant garment of Michaél,
who, as herald of Christ, appears
to thirstily waiting souls,
to whom the Word of Light shines forth.

Michaél *disappears.*

(*stepping down to address the audience*)
You, pupils of spirit-knowledge,
take Michaél's beckoning wisdom,
take the Word of Love of the Will of Worlds
into your soul's aspiring, *actively*!

(*He falters and begins to collapse.* Ita *cries out.* Wachsmuth *and* Ehrenfried *rush onto the stage and catch him before he falls, then help him to his bed.*)

Scene 6: The Abyss

DR. STEINER: Before Germany plunges into the abyss, our friends there will need help and guidance, especially the young people in Berlin. But my physical condition makes travel to Germany impossible, and even an *intimate* gathering would be out of the question.

(*He gets into bed.* EHRENFRIED *covers him with a blanket.* ITA *brings him a writing tray. They exit.*)

(MARIE's *lodgings in a town in Germany.* SAM *enters with* MARIE *and helps her sit in a chair.* DR. STEINER *is lying on the bed in his studio as if dead.*)

SAM   I can hardly grasp that I can no longer meet Dr. Steiner on the hill in Dornach or in rehearsals— or speak to him—or hear him lecture.

MARIE   It is almost unbearable for me.

SAM   Perhaps we should have canceled this performance tour.

MARIE   No. He insisted that our eurythmy programs must go ahead as planned.

SAM   Well, you can be sure that Dr. Wegman is devotedly looking after whatever is needed at home.

MARIE   Yes, Ita Wegman's spent a lot of time with him! (*with a burst of emotion*) I have put up with what no other woman would!

SAM	I'm sure there's been nothing improper between them.
MARIE	Of course not. He wouldn't think of it. That is not the point.—I have been his closest colleague for more than twenty years!
	(*Lights up on* DR. STEINER, *alone in bed. He sits up.* DEMONS *crowd in.*)
DR. STEINER	Marie will have to carry it all without me. Everything now depends on the selfless collaboration of our members. I've made a promise to the spirit world, and I must see it through.
MARIE	Sam, you once asked what happened to my legs. Years ago, an inexplicable paralysis came into them, and the pain became severe.
SAM	It's so unfair.
MARIE	(*reflecting deeply*) My husband tells me it is not a punishment but a sacrifice.
SAM	Maybe it's also a blessing. It seems to me that your work is greater because of it.
MARIE	How so?
SAM	Without your suffering, how would the arts of eurythmy and speech have developed?
MARIE	Yes. I suppose pain and destruction can also be creative. I have had to do my artistic work through others, because I couldn't move on my *own* feet.
	(SAM *nods and exits.*)

DR. STEINER   (*writing a letter*) My dear Mouse!

MARIE   (*also writing*) How sweet of you to write so often.

DR. STEINER   I hope your legs are not giving you too much trouble—and that Herr Meyer will drive you safely to Berlin.

MARIE   It is still painful to walk, and Herr Meyer has a sore throat. But what about *you*? Are you in terrible pain?

DR. STEINER   I have become quite a demanding patient, but Dr. Wegman is doing everything she can.

MARIE   (*coolly*) Of course. I am sure she is nursing you de-vo-ted-ly.

DR. STEINER   She sends you her regards and takes great pleasure in all your successes.

MARIE   I am sure that she does. We had over a thousand people in Bremen. And Hamburg was sold out! I think if we kept on touring, we would be the sensation of the current season. My voice is obeying me quite well.

(SAM *enters.*)

SAM   Another letter just arrived from Herr Doctor. (*she hands her a letter.*) Will he still be able to meet us in Berlin?

MARIE   (*worried*) I very much hope so. (*taking money out of her purse*) Here, buy Herr Meyer a warm coat. He hasn't been dressing warmly enough on this trip.

(Sam *exits.* Marie *opens the letter.*)

MARIE

Will you be able to travel again soon?

DR. STEINER

I don't know. Anything disruptive immediately affects my gastric system. A mere visit from anyone is exhausting. Even Dr. Wachsmuth has not been allowed in.

MARIE

Much too much was demanded from you in September, with far too many courses.

DR. STEINER

It wasn't the courses that overwhelmed me, it was the additional demands from the members. And now they are talking nonsense about my collapse. Stories are circulating, creating confusion and bad blood. But my condition cannot be understood with ordinary notions of illness.

MARIE

How *can* it be understood?

DR. STEINER

The link between the higher part of my being and my physical body is no longer complete. Since the fire, my physical forces and my digestion no longer take care of themselves. They only respond when I bring them fully under my conscious control.

MARIE

Do you think you can manage the trip to Berlin? They've booked the Philharmonic Hall for all your lectures there, and they expect a high attendance.

DR. STEINER

I suppose I have to swallow the bitter pill and send a telegram: I won't be able to come. But I hope *you* will be fully involved and that you will meet with the young people there. It would be good if you could remain close to them.

MARIE   Oh, if only you hadn't worked yourself into the ground for the sake of others. Really! (*mockingly*) People asking you what color *clothing* their *children* should wear! There surely has to be some limit to compassion!

DR. STEINER   There are no limits to compassion.

(*He gets out of bed, as if transcending his body* [*through the letter writing.*])

MARIE   I think about you always.

DR. STEINER   (*crossing toward her*) I'm so very fond of you, and I feel deeply how united we are.

MARIE   But karma also brings other people close to you.

DR. STEINER   Well, that is simply the way karma works.

MARIE   I am wrestling my way through to understanding that.

DR. STEINER   Your understanding is a great blessing for me. My connection with others is different; it is only with you that I can think and feel together, confident in your discernment.

MARIE   I cannot even fathom what you are giving to the world. It is of such inexpressible magnitude. But I will be with you there again soon.

DR. STEINER   It is infinitely dear to me when I have you here at home. But I don't want you to make any superhuman efforts to come on the snowy roads. And I couldn't bear it if you cut short your activity there by even an hour.

(*He gets back in bed.*)

MARIE   (*alone*) It causes me deep pain that I have to be away.

(*ITA enters. The studio. Morning. Hammering outside. DR. STEINER sits up in bed, working.*)

ITA   (*feeling his forehead*) Your fever's gone down a little. You must try to eat something today.

DR. STEINER   (*handing her a manuscript*) I've read through the final proofs. There is something essential for the future in this book of ours.

ITA   At last. It is finished. Now you can rest.

DR. STEINER   But this is only a beginning. We have more volumes to write together.

ITA   Yes. In the future.

DR. STEINER   (*handing her a letter*) I've written another Letter to the Members.

ITA   Another one? These are such an unexpected gift for us. But you need to rest.

DR. STEINER   Tell Herr Pfeiffer that I have read that article—

ITA   The one about realizing that you—were Thomas Aquinas?

DR. STEINER   Yes. Tell him I took great pleasure in it. If more such articles were written in our Society, I would have no need to be ill.

ITA   Surely other hearts will also grasp this karmic thread.

(SAM *enters and helps* MARIE *stand.*)

(MARIE'S *lodgings in Stuttgart.*)

MARIE   It is a painful decision, but I will stay in Stuttgart to regain my strength for the conference here. Meyer can drive you back to Dornach, if you'd like.

SAM   I will stay with you.

MARIE   It would have been such a pleasure to be with Dr. Steiner again for a few days.

(SAM *and* MARIE *exit.*)

(*The scene in the studio continues. The hammering grows louder.*)

DR. STEINER   I love that sound of hammering, the construction of the scaffolds, announcing the coming into being of the new Goetheanum.

ITA   In the last few days the whole world has been asking about the new building. The newspapers even want pictures. But you must rest.

DR. STEINER   I have to be able to work again soon, on the model of the interior.

Ita	The studio next door is being prepared for it. But it can wait.
Dr. Steiner	After everything that has happened, if the building had to be interrupted because of my illness, the consequences would be incalculable.
Ita	You still need to be quite careful.
Dr. Steiner	But I am.—Is Dr. Wachsmuth here?
Ita	Yes. Do you really want to allow him in now?
Dr. Steiner	There is no other way. But he has to get used to leaving when I indicate to him that I cannot continue. (*She nods. Wachsmuth appears at the door. A moment of tension. Ita stands aside.*) (*getting out of bed*) Wachsmuth, do come in, please.
Wachsmuth	Good morning, Herr Doctor. I have brought you more books. And the priests are still waiting with their questions.
Dr. Steiner	Please give them this. It's the last of the ritual texts that I promised them. (*letting him read it*) Isn't it beautiful? —Now, I understand that you want to merge the Archive with the Library.
Wachsmuth	(*speaking rapidly, as always*) Yes, I've asked someone to take charge of both. He says he's already overloaded with work, but I. . .

DR. STEINER   (*clasping his hand*) Wachsmuth, you may not *do* such a thing. The Archive is Fräulein Vreede's work. You may not take it away from her!

Thunder. A spasm of pain and exhaustion. He collapses in WACHSMUTH'S *arms.* ITA *rushes forward. Blackout.*

SCENE 7: UNFINISHED

Thunder continues. Stormy DEMON *music. The studio. Night.*
Dr. Steiner alone in bed. Swarms of Demons. Kingsor appears.

DR. STEINER — Every night the battles recur, filled with evil specters. Klingsor is unfolding his whole power against me. (*getting up, surrounded by* DEMONS, *and confronting* KLINGSOR)

O you senseless sorcery of life,
you rise up in the night,
so that demonic forces—
torturing my soul—
spread out, make misery,
and conjure spirit serpents.
You must vanish.

(KLINGSOR *and the* DEMONS *disperse. Music shifts.*
Thunder. ITA *enters.* DR. STEINER *gets back into*
bed. ITA *covers him with the blanket.*)

(*Late night into morning, Monday, March 30, 1925.*
A violent storm rages.)

DR. STEINER — Frau Doctor wasn't able to meet with the young people in Berlin.

ITA — No.

DR. STEINER — I need to speak to her.

ITA   (*taking his pulse*) We've telephoned her in Stutt-
                    gart.

DR. STEINER   She agreed to remain there a bit longer to ad-
                    dress some difficulties.

ITA   Your pulse is a bit faster than usual, but strong
                    and regular.

                    (*She sits.*)

DR. STEINER   You need to sleep.

ITA   I can't make up my mind to lie down. May we
                    leave the light on this time, for the night?

DR. STEINER   Yes.

                    (*He closes his eyes.*)

ITA   (*praying*) O guardians in the heavens, keep this
                    dear life safe.

                    (*Quiet thunder. She approaches his bed.*)

DR. STEINER   Aren't you tired?

ITA   (*moved*) Your pulse is now much faster, and
                    not as strong.

DR. STEINER   I'm not feeling at all bad. I just can't sleep.

ITA   I'll turn the light off.

DR. STEINER   As soon as it's day, we'll continue with the
                    treatment. You need some rest.

ITA   We won't wait for day. (*She prepares a com-
                    press.*) You were so quiet yesterday, sad and

silent—as though you had a difficult problem to solve.

DR. STEINER There is now a heavy weight in the spirit world. I'm needed there. The dead must be prepared for new earth incarnation. And the angelic realms—it will all be different. Have courage. Much courage. Worlds will falter if you do not have courage to accomplish what the future will demand of you.

ITA I still haven't succeeded in completely understanding you. It seems you are already turning your thoughts toward other, mightier tasks.

DR. STEINER I must redeem my promise to the spirit world.

ITA You have made up your mind.

DR. STEINER A heavenly conference has determined the future.

ITA Is it binding?

DR. STEINER Yes.

ITA (*after a moment*) Do you have instructions for your friends and pupils—for the future?

DR. STEINER (*simply and earnestly*) No. I have said everything that they can absorb. They themselves must create the inner strength not to sink downward.

ITA I will remain forever connected to your being.

DR. STEINER Our bond rests on the most unshakable rock.

ITA

In time and in eternity.

DR. STEINER

No force on earth can sever it.

ITA

No force on earth—or in the heavens,

DR. STEINER

. . . now or in the future. My dear Mysa-Ita.

(*He closes his eyes, folds his hands, and breathes his last breath.*)

ITA

Oh, my dear teacher.

(*Thunder.* WACHSMUTH *enters quietly.*)

He's gone.

WACHSMUTH

(*after a pause*) Herr Steffen is gathering people outside. We will announce the news. (*he goes out.*)

(*The storm has stopped.*)

SAM

(*from the anteroom, offstage*) Frau Doctor is here. Meyer drove us as fast as he could.

(ITA *steps aside.* SAM *enters with* MARIE, *who walks with a cane.*)

MARIE

(*seeing him*) How do you know that he is dead? He could be merely meditating and will awaken again later!

ITA

I am a doctor. But of course, you are an experienced *esotericist.*

MARIE

Yes. And his wife.

(ITA *bows her head in deference.*)

MARIE

Draw up the blanket. Keep him warm, in case he wakens again.

(ITA *covers him with the blanket, then steps away.* MARIE *goes to him.*)

(*sitting on the bed, beside him, allowing the reality to sink in*) He's left so much unfinished!

(MARIE *takes his hand in hers. She holds his hand out to* SAM.)

It is still warm. (*she weeps*)

SAM

I knew. I knew that he would not be with us long. But if you think of him with love and enthusiasm, he will hear you.

(WACHSMUTH *re-enters quietly. Then,* ELISABETH VREEDE.)

ITA

(*confiding to* WACHSMUTH, *fighting tears*) He lifted me up. Such sublimity. He wanted to lead me to spirit awakening, to initiation. But I couldn't see. Not enough. I wasn't able to save him. I was too weak. (*she weeps*)

WACHSMUTH

(*giving her his handkerchief*) Quiet. Don't let her hear you.

(WACHSMUTH *steps downstage.* ITA *is left standing alone.*)

(*to himself*) She failed him. She knows nothing and is capable of nothing.

(EHRENFRIED *hurries in.*)

EHRENFRIED   (*seeing* DR. STEINER's *body*) Oh! . . . Oh.

SAM   I know it is still possible for him to accomplish tremendous things in spirit realms.

MARIE   For us, his work has now come to an end.

ITA   (*quietly*) No. I will keep going forward.

MARIE   Our weakness was a hindrance to his flight. It held him back, like lead around his feet. (*standing*) Now he is free.

ITA   We must carry on the work with courage and trust.

ELISABETH VREEDE

And with our hearts.

MARIE   The earth drifts on in shadows,
while Heaven opens to receive his spirit.
Its multitudes rejoice in reverence.
But gloomy night engulfs this ball of earth.

ITA   He will still work with us. We will go on.

MARIE   If only I had come sooner. To speak with him once more.

ITA   In the light of Michaél, we will keep going forward.

(MICHAÉL *begins to appear above, with the spirit of* MISS MARYON. SAM *steps forward and reads the verse that* DR. STEINER *gave to her.*)

SAM

"Our houses may be shattered into dust.
But in the Temple of our body, pain
may grow into a light of soul,
and through the dust and ashes we will bear
a godly flame within our human hearts."

(*Music. The hammering resumes.* MICHAÉL *gestures "follow me."*)

End of play.

Acknowledgments

First and foremost, I want to thank my partner, Robb Creese, for his faithful companionship and critical eye; Dr. James Dyson for many years of friendship and inspiration; long-time acting colleague Laurie Portocarrero for her perceptive creativity, which helped form the script; and director John McManus for wrestling with the storyline, battling with demons, and pushing me toward a theatrically dynamic play. It would not have been possible without them.

Dialogue and situations were drawn and adapted from published works and writings of many people, including Peter Selg, J. Emanuel Zeylmans van Emmichoven, Rudolf Steiner, Anna Samweber, Ilona Schubert, Marie Steiner-von Sivers, Ita Wegman, Hans Peter van Manen, Crispian Villeneuve, Marie Savitch, Margarete and Erich Kirchner-Bockholt, Elisabeth Vreede, Heinrich Eppinger, Günther Wachsmuth, Albert Steffen, Ehrenfried Pfeiffer, Paul W. Scharff, Paul Emberson, Plato, Aristotle, Alexander the Great, and Thomas Aquinas.

Eugene Schwartz, Sherry Wildfeuer, Gillian Schoemaker, and Brigida Baldszun suggested significant anecdotes. Michael Vode provided resource books. Conversations with Christof-Andreas and Norma Lindenberg, Guy Alma, Rüdiger Janisch, and John Alexandra, among many others, nurtured much of the content.

Jane Kosminsky, Eric Swanson, Toni Tunney, Marianna Rosett, Marc Clifton, James Luse, Dorothea Mier, Robert Karp, Stanford Paris, David Johnson, Barbara Renold, Marke Levene, Barbara Richardson, Charlie Burkam, Ted Pugh, Fern Sloan, Sheila Landahl, Lisa Tracy Tabor, Kathryn Markey, David Fairclough, Paul Newton, Jonathan Fluck, Roxanne Leonard, Astrid Radysh, Nancy Mellon, Mariola Strahlberg, Bill Trusiewicz, Gloria Sauve, Annette Swierzbinski, Ellen K.,

Richarda Abrams, Susan Willerman, David Adams, and Richard Ramsbotham worked through and critiqued early drafts. And Gleice Silva, Matthew Merkin, Hazel Archer Ginsberg, Deborah Grace, Susan Overhauser, Amelia Golden, Christine Huston, and Aaron Mirkin kindly encouraged further developments.

Eurythmists Zachary Dolphin and Sea-Anna Vasilas were delightful beacons of light and gracious artistry through many iterations of the script and staging. And Arla Trusiewicz, Andrew Wolpert, George Russell, John Prestianni, Mike Chase, and copyeditor Anne Newgarden contributed to the final editing.

Glen Williamson
July 2024

The Goetheanum, named to honor Johann Wolfgang von Goethe, the great poet and scientist, was built on a hilltop near the town of Dornach, Switzerland. Construction began in 1913 and continued throughout World War I. An all-timber construction, it was destroyed by a fire on New Year's Eve 1922-1923. Rudolf Steiner, the designer and architect of the building, immediately began designing its replacement made of concrete; he presented his model of the second building in March of 1924, and it was built between 1925 and 1928. The building we see today is this second building and is the home of the School for Spiritual Science and the Anthroposophical Society.

Rudolf Steiner was born on February 27, 1861 in Kraljević, Austria (now Croatia) and died on March 30, 1925 in Dornach, Switzerland. He was a doctor of philosophy and the editor of Goethe's scientific works at the Goethe and Schiller Archives in Weimar. He was a spiritual researcher and the founder of Anthroposophy. His initiatives include education, medicine, economics, art, architecture, drama, agriculture, religion, social organization, philosophy, and others.

Marie Steiner-von-Sivers was born in 1867 in Włocławek, Poland (then part of Imperial Russia) and died in Beatenberg, Switzerland in 1948. Well educated and fluent in several languages, she became Rudolf Steiner's wife in 1914. As a close collaborator of Rudolf Steiner's, she developed the new arts of speech formation and eurythmy at the Goetheanum and worked to organize and preserve Steiner's work for the rest of her life.

** All content in these program notes was compiled from various online sources.

Ita Wegman, born into a Dutch colonial family in West Java in 1876, earned her doctorate in medicine from the University of Zurich in 1911. She co-founded Anthroposophical Medicine with Rudolf Steiner and was the founder of the first Anthroposophical medical clinic in Arlesheim, Switzerland. She attended the ailing Rudolf Steiner until his death. Dr. Wegman died in 1943.

Fräulein Samwaller, "Sam," is a friend, pupil and co-worker of Rudolf and Marie Steiner and has also trained with them in their new art of eurythmy. *Note: the character bearing this somewhat fictional name is based closely on several historic persons, especially Anna Samweber and Mieta Waller, but also Ilona Schubert, Margarita Woloschin, Maria Röschl, Marie Savitch and Louise Clason.*

Albert Steffen, born in Switzerland in 1884, was a poet, painter, writer, and dramatist. He became the chief editor of *Das Goetheanum* in 1921 and, upon Steiner's death, the President of the Anthroposophical Society, serving in both positions until his own death in 1963.

Edith Maryon was born in London in 1872 and died in Dornach in 1924. She was a sculptress who studied at the Royal Academy of Arts in London and showed her work there. She was the leader of the Section for Sculptural Arts of the School for Spiritual Science.

Ehrenfried Pfeiffer was born in 1899 in Munich. His book, *Bio-dynamic Farming and Gardening*, written in 1938, was influential, but it was his consulting throughout Europe and North America that proved crucial to the development of biodynamic farming. Rachel Carson consulted him on the dangers of pesticides and DDT when she was writing her seminal book, *Silent Spring*. He died in 1961 in Spring Valley, NY.

Günther Wachsmuth was born in Dresden in 1893 and died in Dornach in 1963. He had a PhD in law and was also an economist. He led the Natural Science Section for 40 years and served on the Executive Council of the Anthroposophical Society. *Note: the character bearing this name also encompasses aspects of his brother Wolfgang and of Albert Steffen.*

Elisabeth Vreede was born in The Hague on July 16, 1879. She studied mathematics, astronomy, Sanskrit, and philosophy at the University of Leyden. She was the head of the Mathematical-Astronomical Section and served on the Executive Council of the Anthroposophical Society from 1925 until 1935.

The Brownshirts were the storm troopers or SA (Sturmabteilung, which means assault division) for Hitler in Nazi Germany. Essentially thugs, they violently intimidated the Jewish population and others in Germany beginning in 1921.

The Munich Coup (also known as the Beer Hall Putsch) was an attempt to overthrow the Weimar Republic on November 8-9, 1923. It failed, and Hitler and the ringleaders were arrested. After serving just eight months, Hitler decided thereafter to conquer Germany by winning the vote.

Thomas Aquinas (circa 1225-1274) was a Dominican friar and priest who is considered a foundational philosopher of modern thought. In the scholastic tradition, he took inspiration from Aristotle and built something completely new, a combination of philosophy and theology, known as Thomism.

Reginald of Piperno, born around 1230, was an Italian Dominican and close lifelong companion to St. Thomas Aquinas. They taught together in Naples. Reginald attended at the deathbed of Aquinas and received his general confession. Reginald collected all of Aquinas' works and was cited frequently in the process of Thomas' canonization which occurred in 1323. Reginald died around 1290.

Albertus Magnus, a German Dominican priest born circa 1200 and died in 1280, was declared the Patron Saint of all who cultivate the sciences, in 1941. He was the only medieval scholar who made commentaries on all the known works of Aristotle. He worked on a project for 20 years to make all the branches of natural science understandable. He became an important teacher of Thomas Aquinas.

Aristotle, an ancient Greek philosopher, lived from 384 to 322 BCE. He studied in Plato's Academy in Athens from about 17 years old until Plato's death in 347. Afterwards, he did research in Assos and then Lesbos, where he worked with Theophrastus, who had also been associated with Plato's Academy. In 343 he became the tutor to 13-year-old Alexander, the son of King Philip of Macedon. Aristotle's writings cover just about everything: logic, metaphysics, philosophy of mind, ethics, political theory, aesthetics, rhetoric, empirical biology, and so on.

Alexander, the son of King Philip II (King of Macedonia) and Olympias (Princess of Epirus), lived from 356 to 323 BCE. He became the king of Macedonia in 336 when his father was assassinated. Alexander, already acknowledged to be a great warrior, subsequently conquered the Balkans, the Persian Empire, Asia Minor, Syria, Egypt, and India. He fell ill after a lengthy banquet including much drinking and died ten days later at the age of 33.

Theophrastus was born circa 372 and died circa 287 BCE. He was a student of Aristotle and became the head of the Lyceum after Aristotle's forced retirement in 323. The academy grew and prospered while Theophrastus, one of the few Peripatetic philosophers to fully adopt all of Aristotle's philosophies, was its leader. Theophrastus brought to Europe Aristotle's more logical writings, the only writings Europe could accept at that time, while Alexander took Aristotle's nature writings into Asia.

Cratylus was an Ancient Athenian philosopher of the 5th century BCE who, according to Aristotle, influenced Plato before he became a student of Socrates. Cratylus was a devotee of Heraclitus and of the idea that everything is in flux. In Plato's eponymous dialogue, Cratylus asserts that words have an intrinsic relation to the things they signify.

The Temple of Artemis in Ephesus took 120 years to complete after construction began in 560 BCE. Built completely of marble, it was one of the largest Greek temples ever built. It was destroyed in 356 BCE – legend has it, on the night of Alexander's birth – by a fire set by the arsonist Herostratus.

Samothrace, a small Greek island, is known for its temple complex, Sanctuary of the Great Gods, where the famous artifact *The Winged Victory*, which currently resides in the Louvre, was unearthed in 1863. In its time, anyone who wanted to worship the Great Gods was welcome to come to the sanctuary, but the buildings for the mysteries were for the initiates only.

Eabani – Enkidu, is known to us through the *Epic of Gilgamesh*, the oldest epic poem yet found. In this story, Eabani comes to know Gilgamesh as a friend, as a pupil as well as a teacher, and finally as a brother. Eabani and Gilgamesh encounter many challenges in the world that require both of their unique skills.

Gilgamesh is the King of Uruk in Mesopotamia according to the *Epic of Gilgamesh* written circa 1250-1400 BCE. Gilgamesh is described as two thirds divine and one third mortal. In his initial meeting with Eabani, he wins a physical confrontation, but is so impressed by Eabani's strength, they become friends. Gilgamesh needs Eabani to interpret the signs he receives from the Gods.

Druids were ancient Germanic initiates from whom the spiritual life of Europe emanated. Druid culture spread over much of Northern and Central Europe around 3000 or 3500 years ago.

Stone Circles, relics from Druid culture, are found in various places throughout Europe, Great Britain, and Ireland, the most famous of which is Stonehenge.

The background notes to FIRE IN THE TEMPLE *were written by Karen Grant of www.whoareyou.blog*

Notes and Reflections

NOTES AND REFLECTIONS

Notes and Reflections

Notes and Reflections

Notes and Reflections